DARK HEDGES WIZARD ISLAND

AND

OTHER MAGICAL PLACES

THAT

REALLY EXIST

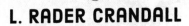

L. RADER CRANDALL

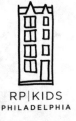

RP | KIDS
PHILADELPHIA

For Roberto and Marcelo,
my favorite travel companions

....

Running Press Kids
Hachette Book Group
1290 Avenue of the Americas, New York, NY 10104
www.runningpress.com/rpkids
@RP_Kids

Printed in Singapore

First Edition: March 2020

Published by Running Press Kids, an imprint of Perseus Books, LLC, a subsidiary of Hachette Book Group, Inc. The Running Press Kids name and logo is a trademark of the Hachette Book Group.

The Hachette Speakers Bureau provides a wide range of authors for speaking events. To find out more, go to www.hachettespeakersbureau.com or call (866) 376-6591.

The publisher is not responsible for websites (or their content) that are not owned by the publisher.

Print book cover and interior design by Frances J. Soo Ping Chow

Library of Congress Control Number: 2019938277

ISBNs: 978-0-7624-6751-8 (hardcover), 978-0-7624-6752-5 (ebook)

IM

10 9 8 7 6 5 4 3 2 1

AND ABOVE ALL, WATCH WITH GLITTERING EYES
THE WHOLE WORLD AROUND YOU BECAUSE THE GREATEST
SECRETS ARE ALWAYS HIDDEN IN THE MOST
UNLIKELY OF PLACES. THOSE WHO DON'T BELIEVE
IN MAGIC WILL NEVER FIND IT.

—ROALD DAHL, *THE MINPINS*

CONTENTS

Dear Reader,

Take a stroll among the shelves of your local bookshop, search your favorite websites, or download the latest app and you're bound to discover a trove of helpful travel guides. They will lead you to the finest hotels, tell you which dishes to order in restaurants far and wide, and explain which shops sell the most authentic souvenirs. You'll find lists of museums acclaimed for their exhibits, maps of city blocks renowned for their architecture, and suggestions of venues famous for their concerts and sports matches. They are all very useful, ideal for the practical traveler.

This is not that sort of book.

Herein lies a guide to our world for fans of the fantastic. On these pages, you'll find places that seem the stuff of dreams—a remote island where dragons roam, distant shores where giants have battled, ancient castles enchanted by fairies—but that are, in fact, very real. They are places you can actually travel to, destinations you can explore, if only you know the way. Many are steeped in myths and legends from long ago that have been passed down over the centuries, while others have histories more fascinating than fairy tales.

It's my wish that you're able to travel to see all the places contained in these pages and—who knows?—you just might discover new destinations along the way. If you do, I hope you'll let me know, for, as you'll see, I love a good story.

To the journey, to adventure!

L. Rader Crandall

GIANT'S CAUSEWAY

NORTHERN IRELAND

On the coast of County Antrim in Northern Ireland, there once lived a giant named Finn McCool who was as tall as ten men stacked on top of each other (although this is certainly huge compared to most humans, it's actually on the petite side by giant standards). Finn spent much of his time each day bellowing insults across the Sea of Moyle at another giant, Benandonner, who resided in Scotland.

"*Howya eejit!*" yelled Finn. "Seems to me you're even uglier today than you were yesterday."

"Easy for you to call me names with the water between us," Benandonner snapped. "Why don't you come over here and we'll see who's better looking after I rearrange your face!"

One day, Finn decided he had had enough of Benandonner's threats and began throwing boulder after boulder into the water in order to build a bridge that would take him across the sea, where he would challenge his foe to a fight. It was hard work, but eventually the path was complete. Finn, exhausted from his labor, decided a quick nap was in order before the battle, and he fell asleep.

He woke to the ground shaking fiercely. Searching for the cause of the tremor, he saw Benandonner stomping his way across the stone path. As he drew closer, Finn's first thought was that Benandonner was one of the largest giants he'd ever seen—the distance really had made him seem much smaller. This was quickly followed by his second thought: there was no way he could beat this goliath in a fight.

Finn ran home as fast as he could. He found his wife, Oonagh, in the garden.

"Oonagh, I've really put my foot in it this time," he panted, out of breath. "I've challenged Benandonner and now he's on his way across the sea to give me a licking. He's the biggest giant I've ever laid eyes on! There's no way I'll win."

Luckily, Oonagh was a quick thinker. "Best not to fight at all then. Come with me."

Finn followed Oonagh into their house, where she wrapped him in a blanket and tied a baby's bonnet onto his head.

"Now go into the bedroom and pretend you're asleep," she commanded.

No sooner had Finn followed her orders than Benandonner arrived, smashing down the door.

"Where's that loudmouth Finn McCool?" he asked Oonagh, who sat calmly by the fireside. "I've come to give him a piece of my mind and introduce him to my fists."

"Oh, I'm sure he'll be glad to see you," said Oonagh coolly. "But, unfortunately, he isn't home yet. If you'd like to go wait in the bedroom, you'd be welcome to, just don't wake the baby."

Benandonner peeked into the bedroom, where the largest baby he'd ever seen lay sleeping.

"*Erm*, takes after his father, does he?" asked Benandonner, sweat beading on his brow.

"Oh, I don't know," Oonagh replied. "The child isn't quite as big as Finn was at that age, but I'm sure he'll have a growth spurt soon."

Benandonner thought his rival hadn't seemed that large from across the water, but if this was the size of his offspring, then Finn must be enormous.

"Thank you, ma'am, but I'll be going now," said Benandonner sheepishly, and he backed out of the house with a bow, then took off running toward the bridge, smashing it as he went so that Finn could not follow him.

"He's gone!" Oonagh called to Finn as she watched Benandonner sprint off into the distance. "I'd say you owe me one."

"That I do, dear," said Finn, breathing a sigh of relief. He vowed not to go around picking fights anymore and he never rebuilt the stone bridge. But you can go and stand on its remnants—forty thousand black basalt columns that look like stepping-stones leading away from the shore toward Scotland, then vanishing beneath the waves.

SKELETON COAST

NAMIBIA

Along the Namibian coast lies a place where many have arrived but few have departed. Portuguese sailors dubbed it the "Gates of Hell," the local Bushmen have called it "the land God made in anger," and as Swedish explorer Charles John Andersson once put it, "Death would be preferable to banishment in such a country."

Welcome to the Skeleton Coast. Consider yourself warned.

This desolate, 311-mile stretch of sand is the graveyard of more than a thousand ships. A nightmarish combination of punishing waves and thick, gray fog—caused by the mixing of cold waters with the warm air of the Namib Desert—make for terrible conditions for any vessel, and many have had their hulls ripped open by underwater hazards or have run aground after losing their bearings in the pea-soup-like mist. The shore is just as unwelcoming, and it's hard to imagine a more lamentable fate than enduring the sinking of your ship and a swim through shark-infested waters, only to find yourself lost in a sea of giant sand dunes populated with desert lions, brown hyenas, and jackals.

As you have likely guessed, dear readers, the Skeleton Coast did not get its name because people survived.

To visit this wilderness, travelers must pass through an entrance marked with a pair of skulls and crossbones. Look in any direction and the expanses of yellow sand stretch to the horizon, interrupted only by the hulking wrecks of the ill-fated liners and freighters that appear out of the desert like steel ghosts rising from the grave. Whalebones and seal skeletons pepper the beach, and it's not uncommon to come across a human skull or femur, too. The wind changes the landscape constantly so that new remains are uncovered while others are buried forever.

And the dunes have one last secret: When the conditions are just right, the desert hums. The air moves through the ancient grains of sand and a low rumble builds to a roar, as if a collective complaint rising from all the souls trapped forever on the Skeleton Coast.

TAJ MAHAL

INDIA

There once lived a ruler called Shah Jahan. He was the fifth emperor of the powerful Mughal dynasty, which controlled much of the northern part of India from the early sixteenth century to the late eighteenth century. Shah Jahan was a born romantic who adored art, delighted in design and architecture, and relished poetry. Most of all, he cherished his wife, Arjumand Banu Begum, who was nicknamed Mumtaz Mahal, which means "Chosen One of the Palace." They were married for nineteen happy years, but in 1631, during the birth of their fourteenth child, she tragically passed away.

Shah Jahan was devastated. He locked himself away in his rooms for a year, and when he finally emerged, his hair having turned white from grief, he declared he would construct the finest mausoleum the world had ever seen. Built along the bank of the Yamuna River in Agra, it would be called "Taj Mahal" as a tribute to his lost love.

It was an ambitious project. More than 20,000 masons, stonecutters, painters, dome builders, calligraphers, and construction workers from across the globe were enlisted, as were 1,000 elephants. Created from white marble and decorated with semiprecious gemstones like jade, amethyst, and turquoise, as well as 8,818 pounds of gold, it rose up 240 feet, was surrounded by lush gardens, and featured a giant reflecting pool. It took more than two decades to complete and was finally finished in 1653.

As Shah Jahan had hoped, it was among the most magnificent buildings ever created, but his obsession with its construction had distracted him from his duties as a ruler and his son seized power. The fifth emperor lived out the rest of his days in his rooms at Agra's Red Fort, gazing out his window across the river at the incredible monument he had made for love. When he finally passed away in 1666, his own funeral was not the grand procession you might expect for a former emperor. He was taken quietly by boat to the Taj Mahal and laid to rest beside his beloved Mumtaz.

Today, the Taj Mahal is considered one of the New Seven Wonders of the World and is visited by millions of people each year, who explore its ornate interiors and stroll the beautiful grounds. Stay the whole day and you'll experience one of the great building's most incredible features: as the light changes its color shifts—rose-hued with the sunrise, bright white at midday, and golden orange when the sun sets.

PREDJAMA CASTLE

SLOVENIA

Erazem Lueger felt rather pleased with himself as he looked down over his castle walls at the enemy camp below.

"Idiots," he said with a chuckle. The breath from his laughter turned white in the winter air and a mischievous grin spread across his weathered face.

A year and a day had passed since the siege on his castle had begun, and his rivals had nothing to show for it save a few errant hits with the catapult. Erazem, meanwhile, was flourishing. He'd grown to enjoy the life of a brigand, robbing the caravans of wealthy noblemen traveling under Habsburg banners and passing the plunder on to the needy. He'd added plenty of gold to his own pockets, too.

He thought back to over a year ago, when he'd raced home across the snow-covered countryside after killing a commander of the Imperial army at the Vienna Court. The man had deserved it, of course, insulting the memory of Erazem's friend like he had, but his death had brought the wrath of Frederick III, the Holy Roman Emperor himself, to bear, and so Erazem had fled to the safest place he knew of: his family estate, Predjama Castle.

The fortress was the largest of its kind in the world, fortified by its position in the center of a 400-foot-high cliff. Behind the castle, a cavern housed a network of secret tunnels that allowed Erazem and his men to sneak in and out undetected to replenish supplies. It had proved to be the perfect base for his exploits, and as Erazem

watched the sun set on another day of his triumphant standoff, he headed off to bed safe in the knowledge Predjama had proved itself impenetrable.

As darkness fell, Gaspar Ravbar, the leader of the battalion tasked with bringing Erazem to justice, felt his spirits fall, too. Every attempt to penetrate Predjama's walls had failed, as had his plan to starve Erazem out of hiding. Not only did the blaggard seem to have a limitless supply of food for his own men, he even had enough to taunt Gaspar's army by throwing cherries over the castle walls, the tiny fruit pinging against their armor in the most undignified way. Gaspar had no idea how Erazem was doing it, but what he did know was that his men could not continue much longer, and the thought of ending his mission in failure left a bitter taste in his mouth.

He had but one hope. His spies had made contact with one of Erazem's men who was willing to accept a bribe. The man had told them about a weak spot in the castle's infrastructure: the bathroom. The informant would light a candle to alert Gaspar's men the moment Erazem was, for lack of a better word, in position, and the army could unleash its weapons, bringing the walls down and thereby crushing anyone on the toilet.

It was not, Gaspar admitted, the most dignified of plans. But he believed it could work. He needed it to work. His men were discouraged, freezing, and longing for home and could not endure many more days of deadlock. Looking out across the bleak and bitterly cold landscape, he knew he couldn't either. Gaspar cast his eyes upward to Predjama's towers and hoped tomorrow would bring the golden flicker of a flame.

The next day, Erazem woke up in an excellent mood. He rose and dressed, then took his usual morning stroll along the castle walls to bask in the sight of his frozen foes below. "Good morning, you plague sores!" He laughed, although he did pity them slightly. Erazem was certain he could keep the standoff going, years longer if need be.

Today, though, it was time to make his way out through the cave's tunnels to intercept a caravan of rich travelers and relieve them of their treasures. He stroked his beard at the thought of the upcoming ambush, his eyes glittering like the riches he was sure to steal. Then his stomach gurgled. "Too much wine and mutton," he said to himself and headed for the loo. Perhaps he'd send the leftovers from last night's feast down to his enemies to really get that nincompoop Gaspar's blood boiling. Then he closed the bathroom door and sat down, the sound of cannon fire erupting beyond the castle walls.

And that, dear readers, is how the fifteenth-century robber knight Erazem of Predjama met his end. But Predjama Castle still stands, and you can explore the hidden cave passages Erazem and his men used, search the attic filled with armor and medieval weapons, and even visit the torture chamber. Just be on the lookout for any lit candles before you use the bathroom.

RAPA NUI
(EASTER ISLAND)

CHILE

Long ago on the Polynesian island of Hiva, a soothsayer named Hau-Maka woke from a terrible dream. In it, the deity Make-Make had shown him the destruction of his homeland. The island sank, lost to the unfathomable depths of the ocean. But Hau-Maka had also been shown his people's salvation: a new island far across the water, mysterious and isolated, which he'd been given directions to. The dream still fresh in his mind, he quickly wiped the sleep from his eyes and ran to tell Hiva's chief Hotu Matu'a about his vision.

Hotu Matu'a sent a scouting party of seven to find the island of Hau-Maka's dream, and, after they reported back that it did indeed exist, he gathered his family and followers and began the journey, using the stars to navigate the vast ocean in double-hulled canoes loaded with plants, food, water, animals, and everything else they would need to create a new life.

After many weeks on the water, they finally spotted the island's cliffs rising up out of the South Seas and landed on the palm-lined white sand of Anakena Beach, which was exactly as Hau-Maka had described it. Hotu Matu'a became the first *ariki mau*, or leader in their new home, which became known as Rapa Nui, as did its people. Many centuries later it would take on a second name, Easter Island, given for the day Dutch explorer Jacob Roggeveen first laid eyes on it in 1722.

It's incredible anyone was able to find Easter Island at all. With the coast of South America more than 2,000 miles to the east and the closest populated land more than 1,100 miles to the west, Easter Island is the most remote inhabited place on earth. And though it's also small, just 14 miles long by 7 miles wide, there's lots to see.

Throughout the island are more than 900 giant stone statues known as *moai*, distinctively carved with elongated heads, stiff arms, and paunchy bellies. Some tower nearly 30 feet tall and weigh over 80 tons. No one is quite sure how the statues were moved into place given their enormous size. Legend says the island's priests once used a power called *mana*, which enabled the statues to walk to their current locations. Others think the Rapa Nui artisans moved them with wooden sledges.

Easter Island is also home to extinct volcanoes you can explore: Rano Raraku, where the stone used to create *moai* was quarried, and Rano Kau, a giant crater with the ancient ceremonial village of Orongo built into its slope. It was here that members of the local tribes used to compete to become *Tangata Manu*, the Birdman, a position that came with privileges and power. The competition was tough, involving a swim across shark-infested waters to collect spring's first sooty tern's egg from the offshore isle of Motu Nui, then a swim back to Rapa Nui to scale the sea cliff and race back to Orongo, where the winner was declared. Although this contest hasn't taken place in more than 150 years, Birdman petroglyphs dot the island and the competitive spirit is still celebrated each February during *Tapati*, a festival with events like canoe and horse racing, dancing, swimming, and *haka pei*, a race down the grassy mountain slopes on toboggans made from banana trees.

DINAS EMRYS

WALES

During the fifth century in the beautiful Welsh land of Snowdonia, the Celtic king Vortigern, on the advice of his twelve wisest advisers, decided to build a fortress on the mountain overlooking what is now Llyn Dinas. It would be, his counselors assured him, the perfect place to seek protection from his enemies. Vortigern ordered all the necessary supplies one needs when constructing a castle—stones, timber, and some lovely velvet curtains—and set his carpenters, masons, and artificers to task. The first day proved very productive, and, as the sun set, Vortigern felt a deep sense of satisfaction at having so successfully watched other people do very hard work.

But when the group returned the next morning, they found everything they had done the day before had been destroyed and the rest of the building materials ruined.

"Wise advisers!" King Vortigern yelled, and the dozen men were quickly by his side. "Any thoughts on where the castle we started yesterday may have gone?" he asked impatiently.

The men did not have any answers, but insisted the hillock was still the best spot for a castle and that they ought to begin again.

"Okay," said the king. "So long as you're sure, reorder the stones, the timber, and the velvet curtains."

The materials arrived and once again the carpenters, masons, and artificers set to work. They got even more done this day than the last, and everyone went to sleep optimistic that the citadel would be finished in no time.

But when they woke up and returned to the site, their work had once again been destroyed, as had the building materials.

"Advisers!" King Vortigern yelled, dropping the *wise,* as he was seriously beginning to question their intelligence. The men hurried over, a bit sheepishly this time. "Do you know why the castle we started *again* yesterday has fallen apart?"

The men were, frankly, confused, but rather than say so, they insisted that this spot above all others was best for the fortress, and so once again new materials

were ordered (although, much to the king's dismay, his suppliers had run clean out of velvet curtains) and the work restarted. And once again, when the new day dawned, all progress had been undone.

The twelve counselors were summoned a third time by their now-livid king, but luckily, they'd spent the night concocting a plan.

"You see, Your Majesty, what we'd, *erm*, neglected to mention is that we'll need a boy born of magic to sacrifice," sputtered the first wise man as the king glared at him, his face red with rage.

"Yes!" piped up a second adviser. "We'll sprinkle his blood around and that will surely fix the problem."

The king looked at his council and thought, not for the first time, about throwing them all into the lake. But, he reasoned, they had been right in other instances, and so he took their advice and sent messengers across the land in search of the boy.

They returned with a child named Myrddin Emrys, who was no ordinary boy, but one filled with supernatural power. He was also exceedingly clever and, upon being presented to the king, demanded to know why he'd been brought so far from his home.

"Well, we've had a bit of a construction problem," the king answered. "And my wisest advisers assure me that by putting you to death and sprinkling some of your blood around, our troubles will be solved, and I can finally build my castle."

Saying it out loud, the king could hear just how strange a plan this was, but he tried to look resolute in front of his prisoner.

"Before I'm killed, may I ask to see these advisers of yours?" Myrddin asked, stifling a laugh.

The king raised his eyebrows at the child's impertinence, but, his curiosity piqued, he clapped his hands and his advisers soon arrived.

"How, exactly, did you hear that spreading my blood around would make this site more fit for your fortress?" demanded the boy.

The wise men shuffled uncomfortably in place, each waiting for another to respond. When no one spoke, Myrddin continued.

"Perhaps you could tell me what lies beneath this ground, then?"

The twelve wise men looked around at each other, eyes narrowed as they thought.

"Um, tree roots?" guessed one.

"Dirt," another whispered, uncertain.

"Very small rocks!" proclaimed a third, sure he'd gotten it right.

"ENOUGH!" screamed the king, and the group was silent. "Perhaps, boy, you might enlighten us?"

"Of course, King," he said. "Beneath our feet is a pool, but I'd like you to see for yourselves what's within it. And for that we need to dig."

The king looked at his wise men and, deciding once and for all that they were a pack of blithering idiots, ordered them to dig where the boy commanded. They fell on their knees and began to scrape away the earth, wondering how they'd gone so quickly from ordering the child killed to performing manual labor on his behalf.

Finally, they came across the underground pool Myrddin had spoken of and in it were two sleeping dragons, one red and one white. As the sun set, the beasts woke up and began to fight, shaking the earth with such force it was soon clear why anything built on the ground above would be shattered. It was a fierce battle, but the red dragon bested the white one, who flew off into the night, never to return.

The king and his men were astonished and stood, mouths agape, as the red dragon curled up and settled itself back to sleep in the pit.

"That should solve your building trouble," said Myrddin smugly. "King, this is an omen. The white dragon who fled represents your opponents and the victorious red dragon, you."

This, of course, is exactly the sort of thing kings love to hear. The citadel was named Dinas Emrys after the boy who, as you may have guessed, was permitted to live. And live he did, harnessing his magical powers to become one of the greatest and most famous wizards of all time: Merlin. The Red Dragon of Wales, *Y Ddraig Goch*, became the symbol of kings and still graces the Welsh flag today.

It's an easy hike through the countryside to reach the remnants of Dinas Emrys. If you're skeptical, consider that the site was examined by archaeologists, who discovered the fort's walls had indeed been rebuilt several times. They also found evidence of an ancient pool where, for all we know, the red dragon still sleeps, awaiting the next child who will discover him.

PIG BEACH

BAHAMAS

Once upon a time, the turquoise bays of the Caribbean Sea were bustling with pirate ships hopping from one island to the next in search of treasure. It was a grand life aboard for the buccaneers. That is, of course, unless a hurricane came their way.

"A storm's a-brewin!" came the call from the lookout of one ill-fated ship. The rain and the wind streaked across the sails, the thunder and lightning roared, and the waves grew larger and larger. Try as they might to navigate the perilous weather, the ship succumbed and was wrecked, all the souls sent to watery graves.

Except for a few unusual passengers.

The pirates kept a pack of pigs aboard as pets—or food, should it become scarce. Preferring not to be made a meal of, the swine seized their chance and, as the ship rocked to and fro, slipped over the bow into the ocean. They were delighted to discover they could swim (they'd never thought to try before), and so they pushed their potbellies through the tempestuous sea as fast as their stout legs would allow. At last, they arrived on an island, and, as they felt the white sand beneath their hooves and saw the lush green jungle in the distance, the pigs knew they'd found a place they could call home.

The swine's descendants, about twenty pigs and piglets, are still on Big Major Cay in the Exumas, a chain of 365 islands in the Bahamas. They spend their days basking in the sun on the beach or snoozing under the shade of the cay's almond trees. The rest of the island is uninhabited, but they're happy to have visitors (apart from hungry pirates) and greet guests who arrive by boat with grunts as they show off their swimming skills in the bright blue bay, their snouts held proudly in the air.

WAITOMO GLOWWORM CAVES

NEW ZEALAND

There are no darker places than the tunnels and caverns that snake their way through the belly of the earth, subterranean spaces sunlight has never touched, where the blackness is so impenetrable you couldn't even see your hand if it were just in front of your face. Few humans dare to venture into these unknown labyrinths beneath the ground and yet, over a hundred years ago, a chief of the Maori people of New Zealand named Tane Tinorau and an English surveyor, Fred Mace, boarded a simple raft of flax stems and, with only the flicker of candlelight and insatiable curiosity as their guides, floated along a stream into the mouth of an unexplored cave on the North Island.

Using poles to propel themselves through the water, they traveled deeper and deeper underground until, suddenly, they found themselves in a grotto beneath what appeared to be the night sky. Looking more closely, they realized the sparkling pinpricks of light they'd mistook for stars were actually thousands of tiny glowworms clinging to the cave's ceiling, their bioluminescent bodies glowing in the dark like fairy lights.

They were enchanted, and, heartened by the room of glittering creatures, the pair pushed on until they came to an embankment, where they left the raft to explore the lower levels of the cave on foot. There, they uncovered vast spaces filled with limestone stalactites and stalagmites that looked like giant sandcastles hanging from the ceiling and jutting up from the floor.

They returned many times to explore the cave, and eventually Tane Tinorau and his wife Huti began leading others through this fascinating world beneath the ground. Today, the cave still welcomes visitors, and many of its guides are the direct descendants of Chief Tinorau, who continue his legacy of shepherding the curious through the tunnels on a boat ride beneath the sparkling glowworm ceiling, which still shines as brightly as it did a century ago, like a starry night without end.

TABLE MOUNTAIN

SOUTH AFRICA

Jan Van Hunks was a surly, cold-blooded specimen of a man if ever there was one. He despised children, had no appreciation for things of beauty ("Watching the sunset—what a waste of time!" he'd snarl. "Not like it won't be back again tomorrow."), and should an unsuspecting dog find itself in his path, it could expect a swift kick. His odious demeanor was eclipsed only by his offensive odor, owing to his hatred of soap and water and a belief that baths were for sissies. Some said his unsavory ways were a result of too many years spent as a pirate pillaging his way across the seas, but most believed Van Hunks was simply born a bad egg.

After retiring from piracy, he spent his days skulking about Cape Town and was easy to spot owing to the near-constant haze of smoke emitted from his pipe. Teeth stained a deep yellow and a beard made brown from the nicotine were proof of the hours he dedicated to puffing away. He even made a decent living from it, challenging others to smoking contests that always ended with his opponents handing over their wager as they crumbled into coughing fits.

When civilized society became unbearable, he retreated to Table Mountain, a flat-topped behemoth from which he could see the entire city and the ocean beyond. It was his favorite smoking spot, ideal for reminiscing about the good old days of swashbuckling and sacking villages.

One day, though, he arrived to find a cloaked stranger sitting in his favorite spot.

"Oy! You there. Get a move on. This is my puffing place," raged Van Hunks, kicking a rock toward the stranger for good measure.

But the cloaked figure did not get up. Instead, he said, "I understand that you are the undefeated smoking champion."

Van Hunks, who was used to having his reputation precede him, did not find it unusual that a stranger should know this. "That's right," he said impatiently. "What of it?"

"I challenge you to a contest," the stranger calmly replied. "The winner gets to stay, while the loser can never smoke in this spot again."

Van Hunks was always up for a challenge, so he agreed. The pirate divided his tobacco into two piles, the duo lit their pipes, and began to puff. Hours passed in silence, and, as they restuffed their bowls again and again, a cloud of smoke spread across the top of Table Mountain.

Day turned to night as the sun set behind Lion's Head peak, and still they smoked. Van Hunks was impressed with the stranger's lung capacity, and the stranger with Van Hunks's, though neither admitted it. By now the cloud of smoke from their pipes blanketed the entirety of Table Mountain's plateau, obscuring it from view. Another day passed as did another night, but when the sun rose again the stranger finally threw down his pipe in defeat.

Van Hunks took a long, victorious drag and smirked. "A noble effort, but no one beats me and my pipe. Now, get lost."

The cloaked stranger turned away from Van Hunks, but instead of leaving, he removed his hood, then slowly turned back around.

Van Hunks began to sputter and cough, for he was looking at a face he recognized. It was the face he'd seen on the bow of his sinking ship when he'd survived by stealing the last lifeboat. It was the face that lurked in the shadowy corner of the pub where he'd won a starving man's last coin and used it to buy himself a meal. It was the face he saw in his nightmares.

It was the face of the Devil.

"You didn't think you could elude me forever, did you?" the Devil said. He walked toward the old pirate, his expression a vicious sneer.

The blood left Van Hunks's face, and, perhaps for the first time in his life, his eyes filled with genuine fear. "But I beat you," he trembled.

"But I don't play fair," replied the Devil. His shadow fell across the place Van Hunks sat. He raised his arms and suddenly a storm rolled in, the thunder masking a blood-curdling scream as, in a final puff of smoke, they both disappeared.

Van Hunks was never heard from again, but to this day, whenever the clouds spread tablecloth-like across the top of Table Mountain, you can be sure the pirate and his nemesis are having a rematch.

LOFOTEN

NORWAY

t was the age of the Vikings, and on the craggy Lofoten archipelago north of the Arctic Circle, there lived the rich and powerful chieftain of Borg, Olaf Tvennumbruni. Olaf loved the Viking life. He spent his days sailing about the fjords in his longboat, trading the skins of seals, foxes, and bears, and leading the occasional looting raid. Evenings were enjoyed with his kinsmen cozied around the fireside of his longhouse, his wife, Áshild, by his side. There, over dinners of fish stew, they entertained one another late into the evening with sagas of Norse deities like Odin, the Viking god of war, and Thor, the god of thunder.

The people of Borg both admired and feared Olaf. There were rumors that he was a *hamram*, a shape-shifter, who could transform into a wolf. Others thought he was simply a bit on the hairy side. Either way, no one could argue that he did a good job looking after everyone. There was always enough meat for roasting, enough honey mead to fill everyone's drinking horns.

But there were changes afoot in the south. Harald Fairhair, an ambitious sea king, sought to rule over the entire country. In the late ninth century, after the long and fierce naval Battle of Hafrsfjord, Harald emerged victorious and proclaimed himself the first King of Norway.

Many opposed him, including Olaf's clan, but Harald was a formidable foe. Rather than begin a fight they felt unlikely to win, Olaf, his family, and his followers packed up their longboats and set sail across the Norwegian Sea for Iceland, where they established a new home.

Abandoned, the village at Borg decayed, forgotten for more than a thousand years, until one day in 1981 a farmer began to plow his fields and discovered fragments of glass and ceramics in the furrows behind his tractor. He had unearthed Olaf's Viking village.

Archaeologists excavated the area and discovered ruins of Olaf's great longhouse, which at 272 feet is the longest Viking structure ever discovered in Europe. Today, it's part of the Lofotr Viking Museum, where you can experience what life was like in Borg by setting sail on a Viking ship, trying ax throwing and archery, and seeing artifacts uncovered from the Iron Age, like golden amulets called *gullgubber*.

The rest of the Lofoten archipelago is just as fascinating, with stunningly beautiful fjords, fishing villages, and beaches, where you'll spot whales and puffins. Because of its extreme northern position, the sun doesn't set for several weeks in the summer, a phenomenon known as the Midnight Sun. Hike along the jagged hills, most of which still look the same as they did in the Viking age, and it's easy to imagine the square sail of Olaf's boat on the horizon, returning to his home in the north.

KNOSSOS

GREECE

Avery long time ago in Greece, there was a great war between King Minos of Crete and King Aegeus of Athens. After many battles, King Aegeus and his troops were beaten. To ensure they never forgot their loss, King Minos made a dreadful proclamation. "Every year, you will send fourteen young men and women from Athens to my island as a sacrifice to the Minotaur."

Aegeus was defeated, but his teenage son, Theseus, unmatched in bravery and strength, was unwilling to watch his friends be sent off to slaughter.

"Dad, I'm going to take the place of one of the young men being sent to Crete," Theseus announced. "I'll kill the Minotaur and put an end to this terrible obligation."

"Are you sure?" Aegeus asked. "The monster is ghastly and lives in a labyrinth that's said to be impossible to navigate. Even if you did manage to slay the Minotaur, I worry you'd be trapped in the maze."

"Don't worry," Theseus replied. "I don't know how, but I'll find a way."

And so the next day the Athenian king found himself waving from the shore with the other anxious parents of the tributes as the ship, pulled along by large black sails of mourning, departed Athens.

Too soon the passengers arrived on the shores of Crete, where a battalion of soldiers led by King Minos was waiting for them. Minos's eyes, as black as his heart, looked over each tribute as they disembarked. The last to leave the ship was Theseus. As he marched by the Cretan army, he noticed a young woman about his age standing next to the king. Her face was troubled, sad even, at the arrival of the Athenians, and, as her eyes met Theseus's, she gave him a grim smile.

This did not escape King Minos's attention. "Come, Ariadne," he said to the girl. "No need for my daughter to tolerate this filth." Ariadne followed him, stopping to look once more at Theseus, who returned the gesture with a grin and a wink.

"What are you smiling at, Minotaur fodder?" scoffed one of the guards, giving Theseus a kick before leading him and the others to the dungeon.

As the day passed and Theseus watched the light disappear from the sky through the cracks in the walls of his cell, he tried to plot a way out of the Labyrinth, but he could come up with nothing. Then, suddenly, he heard a sound.

"*Psstttt*, you, in there." It was coming from behind the cell door.

Theseus leapt to his feet. "Who's there?" he asked.

"It's Ariadne, King Minos's daughter," she said in a hurried whisper. "I've come to help you."

"Help me?" Theseus replied with a skeptical chuckle. "Why would the daughter of my enemy do that?"

"My father is a tyrant," she said coldly. "I would gladly help anyone whose aim is to destroy him and that beast in the Labyrinth."

Theseus trusted the loathing in her voice. The lock of the cell door clicked open and there stood Ariadne, holding a spool of red thread in her hand. "Follow me," she said.

The two of them crept out into the moonless night, Ariadne leading the way to the Labyrinth. A mist had settled, making the maze and its towering stone walls appear even more sinister.

Ariadne handed the spool of thread to Theseus. "Tie one end to the entrance of the maze and then you can follow it back." Then, from beneath her cloak, she pulled out a sword. "I swiped this while the guards were asleep. Thought you might need it."

Theseus stared at her, impressed. "Will you still be here when I get back?"

"Of course not," she said, clearly impatient with his lack of foresight. "I'm going to free the others and head to the dock to steal the ship that brought you all here."

"You're coming with us?" he asked hopefully.

"Well, I can't stay here now, my father will kill me." Then, Ariadne gave him a kiss on his cheek. "Good luck . . . what's your name, by the way?"

"Theseus." He blushed.

"Well, good luck, Theseus. And be sure to meet us before dawn—we'll never get away once the sun's up." And with that, she ran off into the night.

Alone now, Theseus took a deep breath and, after checking that the end of the thread was secured, stepped into the maze. He started off slowly, glancing around corners and stopping every few steps to listen for the monster. On and on he went, turning one corner after the next, the spool of thread growing smaller and smaller. He hoped it wouldn't run out before he found the Minotaur.

He needn't have worried. Another turn and he found himself in a room where the massive beast lay sleeping in the corner. The Minotaur had the body of a tremendously strong man and the tail and head of a bull, horns and all. Theseus tiptoed closer, raising his sword as he went. He was halfway there when the Minotaur opened his eyes.

"Come to die early, I see," said the beast as he rose to his full height, twice that of Theseus.

The Minotaur bared its teeth and charged, pointing its horns at the boy's throat. Theseus just managed to dive out of the way but dropped his sword in the process. The Minotaur charged again, and, with nothing else to defend himself, Theseus threw what little remained of the thread at the monster's head. Confused, the Minotaur dodged and in that second Theseus leapt across the room, grabbed his sword and raised it just as the Minotaur pounced on him. The sword pierced the beast's heart and it collapsed, dead.

There was no time to celebrate. Finding his way to the center of the maze had taken much longer than planned and now Theseus would have to run if he was going to make it to the ship before sunrise. He followed the thread back through the Labyrinth to the entrance and sprinted toward the shore, hoping he hadn't been left behind.

As he reached the beach, he saw Ariadne and the rest of the Athenians were still waiting. They hurried onto the ship and set sail for home, leaving the island in their wake.

Of course, Crete is still there, as are the ruins of a once-mighty palace, known as Knossos, which you can explore. Spread across five acres, the palace's thirteen hundred rooms were once connected via a complex network of corridors centered around a courtyard (much like a labyrinth) and throughout, colorful frescoes and pottery depict creatures of all types, most especially, the charging bull.

LAPLAND

FINLAND

In the northernmost part of Finland lies the remote Lapland region where, in the winter, some days pass without the sun ever reaching above the horizon, a phenomenon known in Finnish as *kaamos*, the polar night. It was one evening such as this that a hunter scanned the snow-covered fell, the reflection of the moon on the white landscape illuminating the dark so that it was possible to see for a distance across the frosted plain. The trees of the surrounding forest were blanketed in snow, their branches shimmering with thick layers of ice, ghostly figures standing sentry. He watched as the fog from his breath escaped his mouth and rose up and outward, disappearing into the quiet night. Perhaps this evening would be lucky.

He gently slapped the leather reins and the team of reindeer moved forward, pulling the hunter's sleigh behind them. Their movement was unhurried and deliberate, the bells that usually adorned the harnesses removed so the group was silent, save the odd reindeer grunt. Silence was essential tonight, for tonight they hunted the elusive *tulikettu*, the firefox, a magical arctic creature. Its fur was white, making it nearly impossible to spot in the snow, but as it moved across the frosty ground its tail created a fantastic green spark that traveled up into the northern sky and danced across the heavens. The light was known as *revontulet*, the fox fires, and it was said that anyone who caught the fox would be blessed with luck and fame. The hunter had already traveled three *poronkusema*—a useful measurement of distance used by the Sámi people that gauged how far a reindeer could travel without having to stop to pee—and he estimated his animals could do several more before they would have to turn back.

Suddenly, a spark.

It appeared on the edge of the forest for a split second and was gone, but the hunter was certain he'd seen it. He guided the sleigh closer to the woods, slowly, slowly, so as not to frighten the animal. There between the pines was a pair of glowing eyes

that surveyed the fell before coming to rest on the hunter and his sleigh. There was a moment, a glorious second of time, when the hunter was overcome by a feeling of good fortune as the firefox's stare reached him.

Then the creature hissed and retreated into the woods, and the hunter slapped the reins harder, the reindeer breaking into a run. The man watched with delight as the path of the animal became clearly marked by a trail of arctic fire, the ethereal, emerald light zigzagging through the trees. Faster and faster they went until, finally, they broke through the woods and arrived at another open fell. The hunter could see the fox hurrying through the snow at an incredible speed, running directly toward a great drop-off. He smiled—for now he had the creature trapped—and he pushed the sleigh forward until the fox was at the edge. Incredibly, the fox leapt into the air and then kept moving upward, dancing through the sky, the marvelous light following, casting a glow on the dumbfounded hunter left below. The firefox never was caught, and the lights sparked by its tail can still be seen racing across the night skies of northern Finland (you may also know them as the aurora borealis or the Northern Lights).

You can experience the fox fires, visible across Lapland's snow-covered fells on about two hundred nights of the year, by dogsled, on cross-country skis, or on snowshoes. There are as many reindeer as people there, so you're bound to see herds of the creatures—easy to spot thanks to their enormous antlers—traveling together. At the end of the day, you can curl up for the night in a glass igloo, designed specifically for the purpose of providing a cozy bed beneath the green glow of the fox fires above.

YELLOW MOUNTAIN

A very long time ago in China, there was a deity known as Huangdi, the Yellow Emperor. He was exceedingly clever, inventing all kinds of things, like the Chinese calendar, writing, and even an early form of soccer called *cuju*. But his greatest desire was to create the Pill of Immortality, an elixir of eternal life. He experimented with various recipes over the years, but the perfect mixture eluded him, until one day his travels took him to Mount Yi.

It was a place of incredible beauty far removed from the outside world. Giant granite peaks jutted up so high the clouds floated below them, hot springs with healing powers burbled up out of the ground, and pine trees in strange shapes he'd never seen before clung to hillsides. Surrounded by this land, where the separation between the realm of humans and the world of nature and spirits seemed to disappear, Huangdi finally uncovered the secret to eternal life. He turned into a yellow dragon and flew up to heaven, where he became immortal. Many centuries later, an emperor of the Tang Dynasty issued an imperial order that the mountains be renamed in honor of Huangdi and his incredible feat, and so they became known as Huangshan, Yellow Mountain, forever after.

Though Huangdi's secret to immortality remains elusive, Yellow Mountain has nevertheless transformed many visitors—into poets, painters, and storytellers, compelled to try to capture the beauty of the place. Sixty thousand steps carved into the mountainsides, some of which are thought to be more than a thousand years old, take visitors up and down peaks with fanciful names like Lotus Blossom, Heavenly Capital, and Bright Summit, along footpaths, across bridges, and through tunnels.

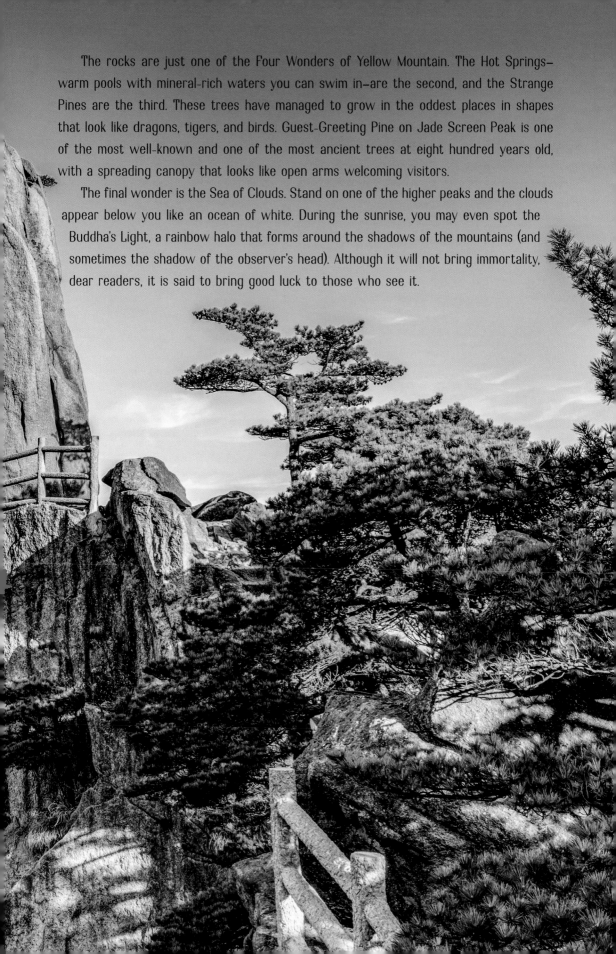

The rocks are just one of the Four Wonders of Yellow Mountain. The Hot Springs—warm pools with mineral-rich waters you can swim in—are the second, and the Strange Pines are the third. These trees have managed to grow in the oddest places in shapes that look like dragons, tigers, and birds. Guest-Greeting Pine on Jade Screen Peak is one of the most well-known and one of the most ancient trees at eight hundred years old, with a spreading canopy that looks like open arms welcoming visitors.

The final wonder is the Sea of Clouds. Stand on one of the higher peaks and the clouds appear below you like an ocean of white. During the sunrise, you may even spot the Buddha's Light, a rainbow halo that forms around the shadows of the mountains (and sometimes the shadow of the observer's head). Although it will not bring immortality, dear readers, it is said to bring good luck to those who see it.

LE MONT-SAINT-MICHEL

FRANCE

Once upon a time in France, a man named Aubert, who was the bishop of Avranches, had a dream. In it he was visited by the archangel Michael, leader of all the angels.

"Aubert," he whispered, a glowing golden light surrounding him. "Great news! I've come to tell you that you've been chosen to build me a sanctuary on Mont-Tombe." Michael launched into a lengthy speech about the sanctuary he envisioned, describing it in great detail. When he was finished, he smiled, angelically of course, fluttered his wings, and disappeared.

When Aubert woke, he was despondent. Mont-Tombe was a rocky outcrop in the bay, and building anything there would be a formidable task. The island was incredibly difficult to access because it was surrounded by quicksand and fast-rising tides. It was also populated by Celtic Druids, who surely wouldn't take kindly to the change. Why on earth would an archangel pick such a challenging place for an oratory? Perhaps he'd imagined Michael's visit. He hoped so. Aubert decided to go about his business and put the dream out of his mind.

But when he fell asleep the next night, Michael appeared again. He crossed his arms, looking less than pleased, his golden glow now pulsing with frustration. "I thought I was pretty clear about wanting that sanctuary built," he said firmly. "And I've chosen you to do it. Most people would consider it an honor to be asked, you know."

But the bishop just stared, his mouth agape at the sight of the angel.

Michael turned his gaze upward and sighed. "For Heaven's sake," he muttered. He looked back at his awestruck disciple and decided to switch tactics, patiently walking him through the description of the oratory again. "Look, I know you can do it," he said, his tone softened. "You're my guy, Aubert." Then he flapped his angel wings and was gone.

Aubert was now truly distressed because this second visit surely couldn't have been a figment of his imagination. Michael wanted that sanctuary, and he wanted it soon. Aubert knew it was unwise to refuse an angel of Michael's stature, but still he hesitated. He liked his simple life and had no desire to undertake an ambitious construction project. Perhaps if he did nothing Michael would choose someone else or, better yet, forget the whole thing.

But the next time Aubert fell asleep, Michael visited him again, and now he meant business. "This is the final visit I'm paying you, and I'll keep it short," he said curtly, his golden aura crackling like fire. "I've told you what to do and now go and do it. Here's a reminder, so you won't forget." And with that, he reached out and gave Aubert a poke in the head, leaving a small hole in his skull.

Aubert woke—albeit with a bit of a headache—and knew what he had to do. He sent messengers to Monte Gargano in Italy to bring back relics of the archangel to Mont-Tombe and began work on the sanctuary. Soon after, in October of 709, the building was completed and the rocky island renamed Mont-Saint-Michel.

The island became a destination for pilgrims as well as a place where many medieval manuscripts were created and stored, eventually earning Mont-Saint-Michel the nickname "City of Books." Over many centuries, buildings were added and rebuilt until it became a towering, tiered monument attracting admirers from around the world. Atop the highest spire, looking out across the bay where Normandy meets Brittany, stands a golden statue of the archangel Michael. And Aubert? He was made a saint for his troubles and the relic of his skull, a distinctive finger-sized hole poked right through it, can still be seen at the nearby Saint-Gervais Basilica of Avranches.

CHOCOLATE HILLS*

PHILIPPINES

I must begin this tale with a disappointing aside: the Chocolate Hills are, sadly, not actually made of chocolate, a fact I discovered too late, having taken a big bite from them, only to find my mouth filled with dirt.

In the age of giants, it was a well-known fact that the colossal creatures did not care for one another. These towering, territorial beings preferred to have space all to themselves, and so, when one giant came across another, there was bound to be trouble.

Just such an encounter occurred on the island of Bohol, when two giants happened to go for a stroll at the same time, one heading south and the other heading north. They met in the middle, and, upon spotting each other, both claimed the island as their own. They roared out insults so loudly the animals of the jungle fled in fear from the sound, and they stomped their feet so heavily the ground shook.

Neither would give way, and just as a battle between the two began, so did a fierce rainstorm. The torrent of water quickly turned the dirt to mud, and the giants took turns hurling massive handfuls of sodden earth in the other's direction. They fought for days, heap after heap of mud piling up around them until, exhausted, the giants conceded that they were equally matched. Since neither could best the other, neither could stay. They departed the island, leaving a mess of muddy mounds in their wake.

The sun returned and dried the mud, the wind blew seeds that planted themselves in the soil, and, as the years passed, the hills became covered in grass. To this day the blades turn a deep brown color during the dry season so that looking out at the domes—over twelve hundred of them stretching across more than twenty miles—is like gazing across an ocean of chocolate-colored waves.

◆ LOST CITY OF PETRA ◆

JORDAN

Frankincense! Get your frankincense here!"

"Myrrh! You won't find a better price in all of Nabataea."

"Spices! Pottery! Camel food! You need it, we got it!"

It was the year 62 BCE and the marketplace in Petra, the capital of the ancient kingdom of Nabataea, was bustling. A central stop along important trade routes that spanned from the Red Sea to the Dead Sea, merchant caravans—some that extended for over five miles and included more than two thousand camels—passed through daily to barter, stock up on water and food, and marvel at the desert metropolis.

Home to over twenty thousand people at its peak, Petra's citizens were skilled writers, artisans, and architects, with towering temples, monuments, and palaces carved into the pink-hued sandstone cliffs, earning Petra the nickname the "Rose City." An ingenious system of aqueducts captured the rain and transported water from underground springs throughout the city to support lush gardens, vineyards, orchards, and elaborate fountains despite Petra's arid surroundings. Even in death the Nabataeans were impressive, buried in elaborate tombs that rose hundreds of feet above the canyon floor, decorated with giant obelisks and columns carved with mythical creatures such as griffins and winged sphinxes. It was one of the most lavish cities in the world, and for centuries Petra flourished.

But in the year 363 CE, an earthquake, one of the largest anyone in the area had ever felt, shook the ground and half the city crumbled. With all the repairs that needed to be done and with alternate trade routes operated by the powerful Roman Empire opening elsewhere, business dwindled. The merchants moved on to new cities, the caravans ceased coming, and Petra's grand streets were eventually abandoned. The city faded from the memories of the living and went unmarked on modern maps, lost to all except the local Bedouins, who closely guarded the secret of the city in the desert.

More than fourteen hundred years passed, until one August day in 1812, the Swiss explorer Johann Ludwig Burckhardt, who was traveling through Arabia, heard rumors about ancient ruins in the canyons of nearby Wadi Musa. Well versed in Arabic history, Burckhardt believed the ruins might be those of a lost civilization he'd heard about only in legend. Concerned the Bedouins might think he was a treasure hunter rather than an academic, he disguised himself as a pilgrim and asked a local guide to take him to the hidden city so that he might sacrifice a goat in honor of the Prophet Haroun, whose tomb was said to be located on the far side of the valley.

Although the guide was suspicious of the stranger, he eventually agreed and led Burckhardt through a narrow, shadowy gorge known as the Siq. It was full of twists and turns, and the rock walls, which seemed to rise up forever, were smooth to the touch, the jagged edges worn away by centuries of floodwaters. They continued on for nearly a mile until suddenly an opening appeared ahead, and, as they passed through the chasm, they found themselves facing a beautiful building hewn into a sandstone cliff. "Al Khazneh," declared the guide. The Treasury.

At over a hundred feet high, with a magnificent facade of ornate columns and sculptures, it was one of the most impressive pieces of architecture Burckhardt had ever seen. With his guide, the explorer spent the rest of the day taking in Petra's magnificent colonnaded streets lined with one impressive structure after the next (and he did indeed sacrifice the goat). When Burckhardt returned home, he filled pages of his journal with all he had experienced that day. And so Petra became known beyond the desert once again.

Today, you can follow the same twisting path through the Siq that Burckhardt took and explore Petra on camelback. You may even make a new discovery yourself because more than half of the archaeological site's 102 square miles has yet to be unearthed.

DUNVEGAN CASTLE AND GARDENS

SCOTLAND

Off the northwest coast of Scotland, on the rugged, windswept Isle of Skye, there once lived a dapper young chief of Clan MacLeod who fell madly in love with a fairy princess, and she with him. They wished to wed, but when the princess went to the King of the Fairies to seek his permission, he told her it was an impossible match—she would live forever, while the chief was merely mortal.

She begged for the chance to be with her true love, and, finally, the fairy king relented, allowing them to stay together for a year and a day. It was the happiest time of their lives and they had a son together. The days passed quickly, though, and soon it was time for the princess to return to the Land of Fairy, leaving her beloved son and husband behind.

Naturally, the chief was devastated to lose his lady love and fell into a deep depression. The members of Clan MacLeod hated to see their leader in such a state, so they decided to throw a grand party in his honor. The chief had always enjoyed dancing and let the melodies of the bagpipers' song lift his spirits and lure him to the dance floor. Everyone cheered and joined in, and the revelry became so uproarious that even the nanny in charge of watching the chief's son in the nursery sneaked out to the top of the stairs to watch the festivities.

The infant began to cry, but his wails couldn't be heard over the music and laughter from the party. His fussing grew so loud that it finally reached his mother in the Land of Fairy, who instantly appeared at his side. She picked him up and wrapped him in

her shawl to keep him warm, singing a lullaby until he fell back asleep. After placing a quick kiss on the infant's forehead, the fairy disappeared once more.

Meanwhile, the chief called for his son to be brought to him. When the nanny fetched the child from the nursery, the shawl wrapped around him began to glow and the fairy's enchanted lullaby filled the hall.

The words of her song explained that a spell had been cast upon the piece of cloth the infant was swaddled in, filling it with magic. If ever her son or his descendants found themselves in danger, they had only to wave the cloth three times and an army of fairies would come to their aid. It could be used on three occasions and only in the direst circumstances. The song ended, and, from that moment on, *Am Bratach Sith*, the Fairy Flag of Dunvegan, has been Clan MacLeod's most prized possession.

The flag has already been waved twice, once in battle and once to stave off a cattle plague. It is currently ready and waiting for its third use at Dunvegan Castle and Gardens, in the heart of the forty-two-thousand-acre MacLeod estate on the wild and beautiful Isle of Skye. On one side of the castle lie the waters of Loch Dunvegan, while the landward side holds gardens and woodlands. Nearby, along the foot of the Black Cuillin Mountains, you'll find waterfalls that cascade into aquamarine baths known as Fairy Pools. You can explore the castle's grand rooms filled with art and antiques and see the Fairy Flag on display. Just don't get any ideas about using it—legend says that anyone other than a MacLeod descendant who tries to wave the flag will instantly disappear in a puff of smoke.

PONTE DELLA PAGLIA

ITALY

Once upon a time, there was a fisherman in Venice, a city as unique as it is beautiful, its magnificent buildings constructed across 118 islands on a lagoon connected by hundreds of canals and bridges. He was a simple man, content to spend his time casting his nets and selling his catch. After a hard day's work, he would tie his boat beneath Ponte della Paglia, the Bridge of Straw, named for the cargo of the launches moored nearby. The gentle rocking of his boat on the canal and the patter of the footsteps of people crossing the bridge above would soon send the fisherman off to sleep.

But on one stormy February evening, a fierce wind whipped across Venice's canals. The fisherman's mooring broke and his boat was tossed along the waves until he managed to paddle to the bank near Basilica di San Marco.

But no sooner had he secured his boat than a man approached him. The fisherman was shocked to see anyone out in this weather, and was even more surprised when the man said, "I'd like you to row me over to San Giorgio Maggiore, if you'd be so kind."

The fisherman looked across to the island where the stranger wanted to go. To get there, they'd have to cross a wide stretch of churning water. "You've got to be kidding," he said. "We'll capsize before we make it off the shore."

But the stranger insisted. "And I promise you'll be handsomely rewarded."

The fisherman thought it a bad idea, but he reasoned he could swim if he needed to, and he was always happy for extra coin in his pocket. So, the pair set off across the canal. Miraculously, the fisherman found the crossing easy despite the harsh gales. They landed on San Giorgio and the stranger hurried ashore.

He soon returned and was accompanied by a young knight in shining armor. They both boarded the bewildered fisherman's boat and pointed to the monastery of San Nicolò al Lido. After another journey across the stormy water, they arrived and were met by an old bishop, who gave the fisherman a smile as he hopped aboard, too.

"Now to the gates of the two castles as fast as we can," the first stranger commanded.

"But that's out to the open sea," the fisherman, soaked to the bone, protested. But then, everything about this evening had been unexpected, and regardless of the reward he was extremely curious about where all this was leading. And so he struck out toward the mouth of the Adriatic Sea, where he soon saw a sight that turned his blood to ice.

There, on the edge of Venice, was a demon ship manned by evil spirits brandishing swords and spears of fire. At the helm was a terrifying monster with flames for eyes casting the spell that was causing the great storm.

"We have come to destroy Venice and send all its citizens to a watery grave!" he yelled, and instantly the squall worsened. The fisherman could barely see for all the saltwater being sent across the little boat's hull.

But his three passengers stood up as if there were no weather to contend with and cast their hands toward the evil vessel. Cries erupted from the demon boat, which began to swirl around in a whirlpool until finally it was sucked beneath the waves. As soon as the last of the ship had disappeared into the water, the clouds parted and the moon cast a glow across the now-calm sea.

"Who are you guys?" the fisherman asked his passengers, amazed.

"Saint Nicholas the bishop," the old man replied.

"Saint George the knight," the man in armor said.

"And Saint Mark, the patron saint of Venice, at your service," said the stranger. "We thank you for the use of your boat, and, as promised, you'll be rewarded. Go to the Doge tomorrow morning and tell him of how you helped save the city."

"But he'll never believe me," said the fisherman. "I barely believe it myself."

"He will when you give him this," said Saint Mark. And he handed the fisherman a priceless ring from his finger.

The fisherman rowed his passengers back to shore, and as dawn broke he arrived at the Palace of the Doge, where he presented the city's leader with the ring as instructed and told the tale of battling the evil ship.

"This ring is always housed in the Basilica, and only Saint Mark himself could have removed it," the Doge proclaimed. "You are a hero and Venice thanks you!"

The fisherman was given gold and the right to exclusively sell his fish in the best parts of town. He soon grew rich, but he found that he still preferred to spend his nights in his boat beneath the Bridge of Straw counting the stars.

When you visit, you can take a *gondola*, the traditional flat-bottomed rowing boat of Venice, on a trip along the canals past the gothic palaces, churches, and islands of this story to the Ponte della Paglia. There, you'll find a carving of a boat, a reminder of the humble fisherman who helped save the splendid floating city.

SALAR DE UYUNI

BOLIVIA

There once was a girl who had a deep fascination with clouds. She favored the billowing cumulus, but she also found the popcorn patterns of the stratus fascinating, the wispy ghost-like quality of the cirrus haunting. Her favorite thing to do was to lie on the grass in her backyard, stare up at the sky, and watch the white forms drift by, identifying what each one looked like—a turtle, a motorcycle, an old man with a long white beard. She often imagined what it would be like to walk across the clouds, hopping from one cotton-like puff to the next, although she knew it was impossible. The clouds were distant, delicate, and changeable, made of ethereal ingredients like water drops and ice crystals. Not the sort of stuff that could support the weight of a seasoned grade-schooler.

Then one day her aunt, a cloud enthusiast herself as well as a frequent explorer, invited the girl to join her on a trip to the South American country of Bolivia. On the flight there, the girl pressed her face against the airplane window, watching the ground shrink away as they rose higher and higher into the blue sky.

"Don't you ever wish you could jump on the clouds?" the girl asked wistfully as they passed by a particularly impressive cumulonimbus.

"Who says you can't?" replied her aunt mysteriously without glancing up from her book.

The girl stared at her reproachfully. She wasn't a *little kid*, after all. She knew better, and, though she wished it were true, she wasn't about to fall for make-believe. She decided to change the subject. "Can you tell me again about where we're going?"

"The Salar de Uyuni, the largest salt flat in the world," her aunt replied. "It used to be a giant lake back when dinosaurs lived on the earth. But over the centuries, the water of the lake dried up, leaving the salt crust behind. Over four thousand square miles of it. That's more than three times the size of Rhode Island."

The girl turned her attention out the window again, spotting a group of clouds that looked like a witch on a broomstick flying along beside them as they made their way south.

The next morning, after a good night's sleep, the girl and her aunt began the drive to the Salar de Uyuni. It was the rainy season in this part of the world, but they'd been lucky with the weather, and today's sky was the girl's favorite kind: a bright aqua punctuated with fluffy patches of cloud cover.

On they drove until they arrived at the great Bolivian salt flat. As it appeared, the girl found herself at a loss for words, for it seemed as if they had left the earth. The white salt crust stretched on as far as she could see, a thin layer of water from the flooded lakes nearby creating the effect of a giant mirror so that every cloud above had a twin on the ground. Looking out toward the horizon, she could barely tell where the earth ended and the sky began.

"Think you can jump on those clouds now?" asked her aunt. The girl nodded, and together they stepped out onto the flat and began to walk, as if they were strolling across the sky itself, into the blue beyond. They stayed for the whole day, watching as a pair of suns set toward one another and stars appeared, the constellations sparkling above and below them.

IZTACCÍHUATL
AND POPOCATÉPETL

MEXICO

In the time of the Aztecs, there lived an emperor of the city of Tenochtitlan who had a daughter named Princess Iztaccíhuatl, but everyone called her Izta. She was kind, generous, and beautiful and preferred to spend her days with her people than with the nobility at the palace. She was beloved by all, and though Izta had many suitors who traveled from far and wide to present her with lavish gifts and promises of wealth, she wasn't interested in any of them. For Izta's heart already belonged to a brave young warrior named Popoca.

Popoca and Izta courted in secret, worried that Izta's father would not approve of the match between a commoner and the future empress. After everyone else at the palace had fallen asleep, Popoca and Izta would sneak off for long walks together, holding hands and discussing their future.

One evening, when the full moon cast a bright glow, Popoca pointed up at it and asked, "Do you remember the story about the rabbit and the god Quetzalcóatl?"

"Of course," replied Izta. "Quetzalcóatl was starving and could not find any food, so the noble rabbit offered itself as a meal. And though Quetzalcóatl didn't accept, he was so touched by its offer that he placed the rabbit's image in the moon so everyone would remember its generosity."

"Well, I love you so much that I'd happily offer myself to save you," said Popoca.

"I love you, too, but I never want to be without you...and you don't look that tasty," Izta replied playfully.

They laughed and stood in the moonlight gazing at one another.

"You know what this means," said Popoca, suddenly serious. "We're going to have to talk to your father."

"Don't worry," replied Izta. "*Tahtli* will learn to adore you as much as I do."

The following morning, Popoca and Izta went to her father to ask for his blessing so they could be married. As they'd expected, it took the emperor a while to warm up to the idea of his daughter spending her life with a simple warrior. But seeing how happy Izta was and how much Popoca cared for her convinced him to agree to the match so long as Popoca proved himself in war, which had broken out against their enemies.

"When you arrive back in Tenochtitlan, you'll be welcomed as a hero and we'll announce the engagement," said the emperor.

It was agreed, and the night before Popoca left, he and Izta said their goodbyes with one more walk in the moonlight. "This is the last time I will ever leave your side," he promised.

Weeks passed and Izta tried to keep her mind off Popoca's absence by keeping busy. On her daily visits through the city, she was often accompanied by one of the palace guards assigned by her father to look after her. As the guard spent more and more time around Izta, his affection for her grew until one day he couldn't keep his feelings to himself anymore.

"Izta, you are so generous, kind, and beautiful, and I've fallen in love with you," he said. "Will you marry me?"

"Sweet guard," replied Izta gently. "You honor me with your offer, but I am already promised to another, the warrior Popoca."

The guard was devastated upon hearing this, and though Izta had turned him down, his feelings did not fade as time passed. If anything, they grew. He was sure that if she could just put Popoca out of her mind, Izta would see they were meant to be together. It was with this thought that he arrived at the palace early one day and asked to see the emperor and Izta.

"A messenger from the battlefield arrived late last night," he lied. "I am sorry to have to tell you that Popoca has been killed."

The emperor looked to his daughter, whose face had turned pale and whose eyes had filled with tears.

"Izta–" the guard began, ready to comfort her. But he was interrupted when the princess let out a wail so full of sorrow it can only be made when the heart is truly broken. Then she closed her eyes and fell to the floor. Try as he might, the emperor could not wake her and the guard fled in fear.

Soon after, Popoca returned victorious. But as he entered Tenochtitlan, instead of the joyous homecoming he was expecting, he found everyone in mourning. He rushed to the palace yelling Izta's name.

"Popoca!" cried the emperor in surprise when the warrior ran through the door. "We heard you were dead. Poor Izta, well, she…" He couldn't finish the sentence and instead gestured to the bed where the princess lay. "I'm so sorry, Popoca, but she will not open her eyes."

Without a word, Popoca took his love into his arms and carried her away from the city to the top of the highest mountain, as close to the moon as he could manage, placing her gently on her back so the light could touch her face. Snow began to fall over them both, but, true to his word, he would not leave her side again.

Touched by his gesture of love, the gods decided Popoca and Izta should always be together and their story remembered for the rest of time. And so, where there were once two lovers, there are now two volcanoes, and what was once Tenochtitlan is now Mexico City. Standing about 17,160 feet tall, Iztaccíhuatl (which means "white woman" in the Nahuatl language of the Aztecs) is shaped just like the princess and is dormant. It's also known as *la Mujer Dormida* (the Sleeping Woman). Popocatépetl (which comes from the Nahuatl words *popoca,* "smoking," and *tépetl,* "mountain") is the second-highest volcano in Mexico at over 17,800 feet and sometimes spews ash and smoke—Popoca still hoping to wake Izta from her slumber.

GREAT BLUE HOLE

BELIZE

t was a sunny, clear day late in the spring of 1971 when *Calypso*, a 139-foot British Yard minesweeper-turned-research-vessel, motored its way through the turquoise waters of Lighthouse Reef Atoll, part of the second-largest barrier reef in the world, about forty miles off the coast of Belize. Progress was slow. Loaded with high-tech diving gear, the ship was the largest to attempt to navigate a safe passage through a seven-mile corridor of the barrier reef. The path was riddled with patches of jagged coral that couldn't be touched for fear of damaging the delicate underwater ecosystem—and putting a gaping hole in the boat's wooden hull.

Oceanographer Jacques Cousteau watched quietly from *Calypso*'s bridge, his signature red knit cap perched atop his graying hair, his brow furrowed with concentration and concern. Maneuvering a boat of this size through such a narrow passage was harrowing, but they needed all the equipment it held, for they were traveling to a place where none had gone before: deep inside the walls of the Great Blue Hole, a massive and mysterious indigo cavity in the reef.

It was over a thousand feet wide and superstition surrounded its dark, unmeasured depths. Some said it was bottomless, whereas others were convinced it was the home of vicious sea monsters. Jacques had also heard warnings that any boat daring to venture over the cavern would be wrecked, sucked down by some unseen force.

There was only one way to find out, but first they'd have to get there.

Cameras in *Calypso's* observation chamber showed the reef below growing closer and closer, until just two feet separated the keel from the bottom. Up ahead was the trickiest part of the passage, which would require a perfectly executed double turn to avoid hitting an enormous coral formation. The crew began the maneuver—and suddenly felt the sickening lurch of the hull scraping the bottom.

Divers plunged beneath the waves to investigate, but, luckily, they had missed the reef and had, instead, caught the keel on a sandy shoal. With help from its launch boats, *Calypso* broke free undamaged and continued forward until it passed through the coral-encrusted rim. Jacques let out a sigh of relief but quickly turned his thoughts to what lay below as the bright azure shallows gave way to the navy hue of deep water. *Calypso* came to a stop above the watery pit.

The group prepared quickly and soon dove into the water. They made their way past the rim of the reef covered in colorful coral and sea fans, spotting a school of sharks, who, fortunately, were not interested in the new arrivals. Through their masks they could see only blackness below them, and, flashlights in hand, they made their way over the edge of the great underwater cliff, down into the deep.

Dear readers, let me tell you now that they were not sucked down into the center of the earth but were instead greeted by the enchanting wonders of this strange pocket within the ocean. They did encounter sea creatures—the cobalt-colored midnight parrotfish, giant groupers, barracuda, and sea worms as big as their arms—but, even more incredibly, 125 feet down they uncovered a massive cathedral-like rock formation. It had archways and shadowy alcoves and long rock columns called stalactites, some as long as 40 feet. Since they can only grow in places with air, this meant the massive underwater cavern had once been above sea level, flooded long ago when the last Ice Age ended and the oceans rose. It was an amazing discovery.

Jacques declared the Great Blue Hole one of the most incredible underwater sites he had ever visited. To this day, divers travel from around the world to explore the wonders of its ultramarine depths that, thanks to Jacques and his team, we now know to be just over four hundred feet deep, big enough for the Statue of Liberty to fit in and still have room left over.

FAIRY TALE ROUTE

GERMANY

It was the time of year when autumn begins to yield to winter, when the crimson and tangerine leaves of fall are ripped from the trees by chilly winds, when the birds head south, and when it's ill-advised to leave the house without a hat. It was at this point on the calendar that Wilhelm Grimm would usually plan to spend his days off parked in his comfy chair in front of his fireplace, a good book in hand and a strong cup of tea within arm's reach. Instead, he found himself out of doors on a gray and frigid morning, pushing past branches and climbing over fallen trees in the wild, primeval forest of Reinhardswald.

He grumbled to himself about his current situation—and the fact that he'd forgotten his warm cap—until his complaints were interrupted by a voice shouting from the woods up ahead. "Wilhelm, I see something!"

"Is it a *gasthaus* serving a hot meal?" replied Wilhelm, his voice thick with sarcasm. "Really, Jacob, I'm freezing."

There was a hurried crunching of twigs and leaves underfoot and Wilhelm's older brother Jacob jogged into view, his expression that of an excited child on his birthday. As was often the case, it was Jacob who had proposed this expedition, and his enthusiasm for exploration would not be dampened by unpleasant weather.

"Come on, grumpy," he said, giving his brother a knowing look. "We're nearly there."

"Well, stop running ahead, then," Wilhelm huffed. "The forest gives me the creeps even in the daytime."

Jacob rolled his eyes but slowed his pace to match Wilhelm's.

"There's nothing to be scared of," said Jacob. "And you know how these research trips always improve our stories. Remember our visit to the Schwalm?"

Wilhelm had to admit Jacob had a point. The brothers were hard at work on a book of German folktales, collected from local storytellers they encountered across the land of Hesse. As they recorded them, Wilhelm had taken to embellishing the fables with details from their travels to add a bit of extra color and intrigue. In the Schwalm region they'd captured a cautionary tale of a little girl who went into the woods to visit her grandmother. As the brothers had discovered, the young women of the Schwalm wore traditional costumes with small red caps, the perfect accessory for the girl of the story. The shadowy forest that lay on the edges of the rolling hills and farms of the valley—which, of course, Jacob insisted they hike through—had made it easy for Wilhelm to conjure a bloodthirsty Big Bad Wolf to cross Little Red Riding Hood's path.

"Then there was that deliciously sordid story about Margaretha von Waldeck in Bad Wildungen," Jacob continued merrily, and, again, Wilhelm had to agree. The tragic tale of a young woman born over 250 years before them had intrigued both brothers—the cruel stepmother, her jealousy over Margaretha's beautiful ebony hair and milky skin, the girl's sudden death at just twenty-one years of age (from poison, some suspected) had inspired "Little Snow-White," one of Wilhelm's favorite stories in their collection so far.

"There also was that amusing tale about the hedgehog racing the hare on the heath in Buxtehude, which was a charming town," Wilhelm conceded. "And the Pied Piper in Hamelin, leading all the rats and then the children out of the village. That one still makes me shiver."

"So, you see? This sort of fieldwork is important," said Jacob, gesturing to the dense woods around them. "And I think this might just be our best discovery yet."

No sooner had he said this than a clearing appeared and an abandoned castle came into view. It seemed incredible that such a structure existed so far into the forest, hidden away from the modern world. Although it had once been grand, it was clear that it had been neglected for some years. Ivy clung to the ramparts, moss seeped from the castle's exterior, and the whole thing was surrounded by a foreboding wall of thorns.

"It's quite the fixer-upper," Wilhelm joked as they came around the side of the ruined palace to discover a wall had crumbled away completely, leaving a gaping hole in the side. "And it might be a bit cold in winter."

Jacob laughed. "I wasn't thinking of moving in, but when I heard about this place I did think of someone else who might live here," he said, pointing at the turrets. "A sleepy beauty, perhaps?"

Wilhelm knew his brother was referring to the tale they'd heard of a princess that pricked her finger on a cursed spinning wheel and fell into a deep sleep along with all the noble men and women within the castle walls. There, they slept for a century, awaiting a prince's kiss to break the spell, while the world continued on without them. He took in the castle's details, the border of thorns, the crumbling towers. It wasn't hard to imagine that somewhere in the ruins, a court of people frozen in time was hidden.

Wilhelm stepped into the weedy courtyard, where rosebushes had taken over the sides, their blooms gone with the warm weather so that now there were just gnarls of prickly stems, and all at once, he saw the story as he would record it. He turned to Jacob, his eyebrows raised with intrigue. "What do you think of the name Brier-Rose?"

"Perfect," replied Jacob, and the Brothers Grimm made their way back into the woods.

More than two hundred years after Jacob and Wilhelm published their first collection of Grimm's Fairy Tales, the places that inspired them can still be explored along the German Fairy Tale Route. Stretching more than 350 miles from Hanau to Bremen, you'll find the Sababurg Castle of "Sleeping Beauty" fame and the tower where Rapunzel let down her hair. You can hike the shadowy forests where Little Red Riding Hood ventured, stroll the cobbled streets lined with timber-framed houses where the Pied Piper played, and even visit the places where Jacob and Wilhelm lived and wrote. You just may be inspired to write your own story.

KOMODO ISLAND

INDONESIA

In the days when much of the world was still unexplored and no one could be sure what lurked beyond the horizon, an expression was used to warn others off the untouched corners of the earth: *hic sunt dracones*. Here be dragons.

The winged, fire-breathing creatures were fierce to be sure, and the people of yore avoided them at all costs. But as sightings became rarer and rarer, and more and more places were uncovered, the expression fell out of fashion until, eventually, no one mentioned dragons at all. They became myths, fantastic beasts found only in storybooks.

So it was a surprise when, one day in 1910, Dutch lieutenant Jacques Karel Henri van Steyn van Hensbroek, who was stationed in eastern Indonesia, heard rumors about monstrous lizards roaming around a nearby island. Sailors insisted they had seen dragons with bodies longer than crocodiles'. Some said they could spit fire, and others reported they had wings and could fly. Intrigued by the tales, the lieutenant mounted an expedition and headed to Komodo island.

HERE BE DRAGONS!

Landing on the island, van Steyn van Hensbroek and his team quickly encountered the creatures. They took photos and even sent the skin of one to Pieter Ouwens, then director of the Java Zoological Museum and Botanical Gardens. He determined the animal, a giant monitor lizard, was a new discovery and named it *Varanus komodoensis*, Komodo dragon.

Thankfully, these dragons can't actually fly (although, with speeds of up to twelve miles per hour, they can run alarmingly fast), and though no fire shoots from their mouths, their bite is toxic. Komodos can weigh as much as three hundred pounds when they're adults and grow to be ten feet long. They have long, yellow, forked tongues and are covered in armored scales that act as a chain mail of sorts for their rough, leathery skin. Their powerful tails are as long as their bodies, and red, blood-tinged saliva drips from their razor-sharp teeth.

After a night's rest in their burrows, these carnivores emerge to spend their days hunting Komodo's grasslands and mountains in search of deer, goats, wild pigs, or even water buffalo for dinner. The dragons are stealthy, silently tracking their prey, then charging at full speed to use their sharp claws, shark-like teeth, and poisonous venom to take down their prey. They can eat 80 percent of their body weight in one sitting and have even been known to swallow smaller animals whole.

Luckily, they tend to be shy creatures, preferring to keep to themselves, for the most part. But, if you do spot a dragon sunning itself in the sand, be sure to keep your distance—an unsuspecting human could make a delicious meal for a Komodo dragon, too.

WIZARD ISLAND

UNITED STATES

The Klamath Tribes tell of a time long, long ago when there existed two powerful spirits: Llao, ruler of the underworld, who dwelled beneath a great lake at the top of a mountain, and Skell, overseer of the aboveground kingdom that spread across the low-lying marsh country at the foot of Lao-Yaina (today known as Mount Mazama in Oregon). Each commanded groups of lesser spirits who could transform themselves into anything they liked. Llao's minions included monsters such as a giant crawfish who would drag unwelcome trespassers down into the lake's watery depths, while the beings who followed Skell took the form of land animals such as the deer and the wolf, as well as birds like the eagle and the dove.

For many years the two groups lived together peacefully, but one day a fight broke out between the creatures and so began a bitter war. After many battles, Skell of the aboveground lost and his enemies took his heart from his chest and carried it up Lao-Yaina. Llao planned a party to celebrate the underworld's victory and even invited his rival's followers to join them. The festivities began with a game of catch. "For a ball," declared Llao, "we will use Skell's heart!"

Now, Skell's followers knew that if they were able to return their leader's heart to his body he would be brought back to life and so they devised a plan to steal it. As the game progressed, they inched closer and closer to the edge of the woods.

"I thought you were supposed to be a god!" said Deer, taunting Llao. "You throw like a mortal."

"Yes, toss it higher!" Fox chimed in, giving the heart a good heave across the circle.

Not wanting to be shown up, Llao and his monsters did throw the heart farther and faster, with Skell's animals leading their foes ever closer to the forest. Finally, Antelope was standing right on the edge of the trees as the heart sailed toward him. He caught it and, with a mischievous wink, turned and ran as fast as he could into the woods.

Realizing they'd been tricked, Llao and his followers sprinted after Antelope, but he was too fast for them. When he got tired, he passed the heart to Wolf, who ran with it until his pace slowed, then he passed it to Eagle, who flew for hours until he finally passed it to Dove. Knowing the heart was now too far away to pursue, Llao and his monsters turned back, and, victorious, Skell's animals returned the heart to their master. He opened his eyes, alive once again.

"I am forever grateful to you," Skell said to his beasts. "Now, let's finish this once and for all."

Heartened by his return, Skell's army rushed toward Lao-Yaina, tracked down Llao, and swiftly defeated him. Skell took Llao's body to the top of a cliff overlooking the lake, and then sent Antelope down to the shore, where he told Llao's followers a lie: "Skell has lost again," he fibbed. "And to prevent him from coming back another time, Llao has commanded he be chopped up and fed to you, his faithful monsters of the underworld."

The beasts rejoiced at the news. Sure enough, when each part of the body was tossed into the lake, the gluttonous creatures devoured it thinking it was their enemy Skell. "Delicious," proclaimed the giant crawfish, licking his lips.

Finally, though, Skell tossed Llao's head into the lake. The monsters gasped when they recognized their leader and slunk away in shame, leaving the ruler of the underworld's noggin floating in the water. It is still there and today is known as Wizard Island, which rises 763 feet up from the water on the west end of *giiwas*, the Klamath word for Crater Lake, in south-central Oregon. Llao's soul remains trapped in the cliff, Llao Rock, the highest vertical precipice on the lake. When a sudden storm brews, it's said Llao's spirit is visiting the water below, his screams of anger audible on the wind, the waves whipping the shore as he protests his fate.

Fed only by water from rain and snow rather than rivers or streams, turquoise-colored Crater Lake is the deepest lake in the United States and is among the most pristine large bodies of water in the world. When you go, you can hike the trails around its rim or take a boat ride to explore Wizard Island, where visitors with strong constitutions are welcome to go for a dip in the lake's (very cold) water.

TOWER OF LONDON

ENGLAND

Along the northern bank of the River Thames lies a mighty fortress where epic triumphs and ghastly tragedies have unfolded across centuries. Its walls house legendary ghosts, unflappable guards, and a great treasure. This is the Tower of London, and though it's a fascinating place to explore today, in the past some visitors never got the chance to leave.

Built by William the Conqueror, the first Norman king of England, in the eleventh century, the Tower's defenses were gradually expanded until it became a place where kings and queens could be sure they (and their riches) would be protected. Arms and armor were once tested and forged here, coins of the realm were made in the Tower Mint until 1810, and the Crown Jewels—a collection of 23,578 gemstones and royal regalia like tiaras and scepters—are still kept in the Jewel House on full display. Just don't try any funny business. The riches are watched over by the Tower's red-coated guards, the Yeoman Warders, also known as Beefeaters because they used to be paid in part with portions of meat. The Yeoman Warders also watch over the suits of armor and weapons in the White Tower (some of which you can try), guard the splendid rooms of the Medieval Palace (which you can visit), and perform the ritual locking-up of the Tower, the Ceremony of Keys, which has taken place each and every night for seven hundred years (which you can watch).

The Beefeaters are helped with their

guard duties by the unkindness of ravens whose ancestors have lived on the South Lawn of the Tower since the seventeenth century, when King Charles II was told that the kingdom would fall unless there were six ravens living on the grounds at all times. These winged guardians are free to roam about the Tower and meet visitors, though they always return to their perch, where the Ravenmaster feeds them their favorite meal: biscuits soaked in blood.

Of course, this impenetrable castle made an excellent prison, too, and became the final residence of many unfortunate souls punished for their treachery or, sometimes, simply for getting on the current ruler's bad side. Among the most famous were two young princes, Edward V and Richard, Duke of York. The brothers were locked away by their power-hungry uncle Richard III in 1483 never to be heard from again, though bones that some believe to be the boys' were found beneath a staircase in 1674. The section of the fortress where they were imprisoned became known as the Bloody Tower.

During the sixteenth century, when he was displeased the wildly temperamental King Henry VIII had the terrible habit of ordering his wives' heads chopped off on the Tower Green, first Anne Boleyn in 1536, then Catherine Howard in 1542. Lady Jane Grey, known as the "Nine Days Queen" after being overthrown by Mary I only nine days into her reign, also lost her head in 1554.

The ghosts of these and other prisoners have been spotted over the years, making the Tower one of the most haunted places in the world. Whether you believe the ghost stories or not, rest assured that a trip to the Tower Green or the Bloody Tower, especially at twilight, is bound to end with goose bumps.

CAPPADOCIA

TURKEY

The boy was up before the sun, which was very unusual, but then so was the spot he found himself that morning: in the basket of a hot-air balloon. It was his first day in Cappadocia, an ancient district north of Turkey's Taurus Mountains, and he and his family had risen early for a ride over the land known for its strange rock formations and curious abodes.

He watched the pilot fire the balloon's flame and felt the basket lift up and away from the ground. On such an early adventure he was grateful for having got a good night's sleep, though the accommodations, a *cave* hotel, had been like no place he'd ever stayed before. It was one of many guesthouses in the area carved right into the rocks and had actually been very comfortable, with plenty of lights and a snug bed, like spending the night in a luxurious secret lair.

As morning light began to fill the sky, he was delighted to see dozens of other hot-air balloons were also beginning their trips across the valley, and the effect of all the colorful spheres together made it feel as if they were throwing the sunrise a party. Then he looked down and saw they were drifting across a landscape so unusual-looking he thought for a moment they might have traveled to another planet.

There were bizarre rocks called fairy chimneys poking up over a hundred feet from the ground, their mushroom-shaped tops capping off long, spindly stems. In the distance he saw Uçhisar Castle, a towering fortress sculpted into the rock with so many rooms and tunnels that it seemed to be made out of Swiss cheese. There was also Göreme, a group of chapels with evocative names such as Snake Church, Apple Church, and Dark Church, carved from soft volcanic tuff in the tenth to thirteenth centuries and decorated with colorful frescoes.

The boy also wanted to see Cappadocia's underground cities, such as Derinkuyu, which snaked its way through eighteen subterranean stories filled with stables, wineries, kitchens, and schools. Built by its inhabitants more than a millennium ago as a place to hide from attackers, it's thought that twenty thousand people and their animals could live here—and on short notice. He'd read that it had been discovered in 1963, when a passageway to the city was found during a local family's home renovation. Scientists had since uncovered about six hundred more secret entrances in other buildings and courtyards, which, the boy thought, was proof that you never know what you might find hidden in your own house.

They continued across the aptly named Imagination Valley, home to a zoo's worth of rocks shaped like a camel, a seal, a dolphin, and a snake, before the balloon began its return trip. Taking in the bird's-eye view, the boy was suddenly struck by the extraordinary fact that the fairy chimneys and the honeycombed hills had been here long before him and would be here long after.

Then, *bump.* His reverie was broken by the gentle thud of the basket landing on the ground, and, together with his family, the boy headed out for another adventure in Cappadocia, the sun now firmly in the sky.

GREAT SPHINX OF GIZA

EGYPT

ong ago, around 1400 BCE, when the powerful Eighteenth Dynasty of the Egyptian Empire ruled, there was a prince named Thutmose IV who was the son of the Pharaoh Amenhotep II and his queen consort, Tiaa. Thutmose and his family lived in the New Kingdom capital of Thebes, and although the young prince had many siblings, he was often lonely, for even though he was not the oldest or next in line for the throne, he was witty, handsome, and often favored by their father, and this made him the object of his brothers' jealousy and scorn.

He tried to get along with everyone, but his siblings were constantly plotting ways to make him look bad—leaving snakes in the kitchen pots to frighten the palace cooks or wrapping their pet cats up in mummy bandages, then blaming the antics on Thutmose. Their tricks rarely worked, but as he grew older, the prince tired of the endless bickering and backstabbing and so was thrilled when he was offered a posting north along the Nile River at the military base in the ancient city of Memphis, near what is now Cairo. Away from the palace, he flourished, spending his days off with friends practicing archery, chariot racing, playing sports like tug-of-hoop (which is like tug-of-war, but with sticks and a ring), and hunting lions, leopards, and antelope along the desert steppe of the Nile Valley. But he could not escape his dreams, which were often filled with unhappy memories of his days at the Pharaoh's court, and a gnawing guilt that, despite his troubles, the palace was where he belonged.

Whenever he endured a restless night, Thutmose would ride out on his own at sunrise to clear his head. One morning after a particularly bad night's sleep, he lost track of the time. It was nearly noon when he found himself in the yellow sands surrounding the Great Pyramids, built by pharaohs of the Old Kingdom a thousand years before Thutmose was born. As the sun neared its peak in the sky, the prince had to seek out shade in the sweltering heat. He sat down in the shadow of a giant statue, the Great Sphinx, most of which had been buried with sand over several hundreds of years so that only the top part of the statue's head could be seen. Drowsy from his morning ride and relaxed by the sensation of the warm, soft sand beneath him, he dozed off.

Thutmose soon began to dream. He saw himself asleep just as he really was, but suddenly from behind him came an incredible yawn that rolled on as loud and long as thunder. He jumped up and saw the Sphinx shaking its head, awakening from a slumber that had lasted a millennium. Its massive eyes searched the surroundings, then settled on Thutmose, who was awestruck by the sight of the ancient statue coming to life. Then the Sphinx began to speak.

"Thutmose," it said, "behold, it is I, the sun god, Hor-em-akhet."

Surprised at being addressed by name by a talking statue, Thutmose took a moment to soak in just what was happening.

"As you can see, years spent exposed to the elements have been hard on me and I'm now covered in sand up to my chin," the statue continued. "My body, the powerful legs and clawed feet of a majestic lion, must be freed. So, I have a proposition for you. Release me from this prison of sand, and you'll be the next ruler of Egypt, prosperity and happiness your legacy." And with that, the Sphinx once again became solid stone and the prince woke up from his dream.

Thutmose leapt to his feet, mounted his horse, and rode directly for home, where he told everyone of his vision and pronounced himself the next in the line of the great pharaohs. His father agreed, much to his brothers' chagrin, and as soon as he had taken over the throne, Thutmose kept his promise and had the Sphinx excavated from the sand. When the great statue was free from the desert, Thutmose placed a granite slab engraved with the details of his dream between the Sphinx's feet, each twice as tall as a full-grown person and as long as a school bus. He spent the rest of his reign in prosperity, regaling the New Kingdom with stories of the Sphinx's power.

But over time, the sand swept along by the winds reclaimed the statue, the Egyptian Empire crumbled, and the story of the sun god and the prince was buried beneath the grains of the Sahara for centuries more. That is, until a team of archaeologists once again excavated the statue and discovered the plaque with the story of Thutmose and the Sphinx. It became known as the "Dream Stela," and it still sits between the paws of the statue in Giza, where you can go and see it. At nearly twelve feet high, it's twice as tall as a grown person but feels small compared to the Sphinx, which looms to a height of sixty-six feet, while nearby the Great Pyramids rise out of the Egyptian desert.

GÁSADALUR

FAROE ISLANDS

Once upon a time on the island of Vágar, a young man sat waiting on the edge of the remote village of Gásadalur. He could barely contain his excitement, for he'd been selected as the town's new postman, and, as any of the villagers would tell you, mail carriers had to be among the bravest and strongest of all the islanders. They trekked over four miles from their hamlet to the larger town of Bøur and back several times a week to deliver parcels and letters and return with news from the outside world. It was a perilous journey, across mountains and along sheer cliffs, but it was the only route connecting Gásadalur, and, on this day, the young man would learn its secrets from the town's longtime postmaster.

"Good morning!" exclaimed the eager trainee when he saw the old postmaster emerge from the shadow cast by Árnafjall, the tallest mountain on the island. The postmaster merely responded with a grunt and handed a heavy sack to the young man, gesturing that he should carry it as the two set off on their journey. After the pair had walked awhile in silence, the postmaster finally spoke. "It is important you learn the landmarks," he said firmly. "Day or night, in fine weather or in a storm, these markers will show you the way home."

The young man nodded solemnly, and they continued on until the postmaster stopped, cupping his hand to his ear, indicating that the young man should listen. "You'll know you are nearing our village when you hear the roar of the waterfall," the postmaster said as he looked out across the land they had just crossed. "From here, you can see Risasporið, the giant's footprint. It was made long ago by the giant of Gásadalur, who wanted to fight the giant of Mykines, the island across the water. With a running leap, he made the jump across the channel, lifting off with such force that his foot made that indentation there."

The young man's eyes widened at the impression in the land, but he had little time to dwell on the thought of ancient giants as he scrambled along after the postmaster, who had already hurried onward. The old man kept an arduous pace through the misty mountains until, finally, they stopped to rest.

The young man was grateful for the pause—the journey was taxing and the sack heavy, and yet the postmaster showed no signs of fatigue. "We are halfway to Bøur, and this is another landmark," the postmaster said with a touch of mystery in his voice, and he gestured to the large, flat stone upon which they sat. "This rock is called Líksteinurin, the Corpse Stone, because it is the only place on this trail where a coffin can be rested for those who carry the dead away from our village."

The young man gulped, for it was never pleasant to think on death, and the old postmaster rose and continued along the path, which began a steep descent. The postmaster gestured out to the craggy, uninhabited island off the coast. "The last landmark," he barked. "You'll know you are close when you can see the five peaks of Tindhólmur." Sure enough, they soon spotted the roofs of the seaside village of Bøur. The young man sank to his knees in the town square, damp with sweat from exertion. The old postmaster took a swig of ale from his cask and allowed his protégé to catch his breath.

"You did well," the postmaster declared, allowing a smile to form on his lips. "It is not easy to continue forward without complaint when you receive little encouragement, are uncomfortable, and are overwhelmed. You'll grow fitter, but a strong will cannot be taught, and you've proven to me today that you have what is needed to make your way over the mountains when I am no longer here to guide you."

And so the young postman spent his days growing stronger as he navigated the path to and from Gásadalur. Years later, he would teach these same lessons to the mail carrier after him. Eventually, a road was built and a tunnel constructed through the mountains so that today you can drive from one village to the next, but the old postal route still lies along the coast for those bold enough to hike it, the landmarks leading the way.

SHIMANE PREFECTURE

JAPAN

The next time you're tempted to pick on your sibling, think of the Shinto storm deity Susanoo-no-Mikoto who got kicked out of the realm of the gods for playing one too many tricks on his sister, Amaterasu, the goddess of the sun. He was banished to earth, where he arrived in the land of Izumo along a babbling river. Susanoo spotted a pair of chopsticks floating down the stream and, figuring they must have come from a village, followed the water through the countryside until he came upon a home where he met an elderly couple and their daughter.

The mother and father were distraught. Originally, they'd had eight daughters, but every year the terrible monster Yamata-no-Orochi arrived and devoured one of their offspring so that now the only one left was their youngest, Kushinada-hime. Yamata-no-Orochi would be visiting again soon, and the family was overcome with grief.

"What does this beast look like?" asked Susanoo, who, given that he was a god, was not inclined to be afraid of monsters.

"Oh, he's terrible," replied the father. "He has eight fearsome heads and eight powerful tails. His eyes are red like the winter berry and his body is the length of eight valleys and eight hills."

"Hmm, he does sound formidable," Susanoo said, stroking his beard as he thought. "But," he said after a while, "I think I have a plan. Do you know how to make sake?"

"Sake? Why . . . yes," replied the father, scratching his head. He wondered what rice wine had to do with slaying a colossal beast.

"Great. I'll need you to make an enormous batch, and distill it eight times," said Susanoo confidently. "Also, we'll need to build a vast fence with eight gates, and through each gate we'll have a platform with a giant barrel full of sake."

The group set to work and finished the tasks with barely any time to spare before the ground began to shake, signaling the approach of Yamata-no-Orochi.

"Let's make sure the monster can't find you," Susanoo said to Kushinada-hime, and he used his magic to transform her into a comb, which he tucked into his hair so that she'd be safe.

The serpent was as terrifying as described. Its eight hideous heads did indeed have eyes like pools of fire, its eight tails were spiked and dangerous, thrashing anything that got in their path. It was epic in size, its back so gargantuan that it had sprouted trees. As they watched it approach from their hiding spot, the elderly couple grew more and more worried. Defeating the beast seemed an impossible task, even for the storm god.

But Susanoo knew something they did not: giant eight-headed monsters *love* liquor. Sure enough, Yamata-no-Orochi headed straight for the vats of sake, each of its heads passing through the gates to drink deeply. The beast drank and drank until it grew drowsy and fell asleep. Seizing his chance, Susanoo sprung out from hiding and swiftly cut off each of the monster's heads with his sword. Then, he made his way to its tails, but as he went to chop off one of the middle tails, his sword splintered and broke.

Now it was Susanoo's turn to be mystified. What in the world could shatter a god's saber? He reached inside the tail and discovered the

most incredible sword he'd ever seen. He named it Ame-no-Murakumo-no-Tsurugi, which means "Sword of the Gathering Clouds of Heaven" (this sword, dear readers, would later become known as Kusangai and is one of the Three Sacred Treasures of Japan. But that is a story for another time). Susanoo brandished the great weapon above his head triumphantly, then used it to finish the work of dispatching the serpent.

Freed from Yamata-no-Orochi's tyranny, Susanoo transformed Kushinada-hime back into her human form. They were married at the Yaegaki Shrine (which means "Shrine of the Eightfold Fence"), which you can visit in what today is known as the Shimane Prefecture of Japan. It's said that if you place a piece of paper with a coin and a prayer written on it into the waters of Mirror Pond there, the speed and position at which the paper sinks will predict your fortune in love.

The Kumano Taisha is also nearby, a shrine dedicated to the couple (and Susanoo's mother, the goddess of creation, Izanami-no-Mikoto) that's believed to bring visitors good luck in new ventures. At Izumo Taisha, one of the most ancient shrines in Japan, it's said that in the tenth month of the lunar calendar the eight million Shinto deities gather for a meeting to determine the destiny of people. This is why the month is called *Kannazuki* (Month Without Gods) in every part of Japan except for this one, where it's known as *Kamiarizuki* (Month with Gods).

REYNISDRANGAR

T he three-masted ship moved silently through the water, its vast hull cutting through the icy waves like a knife through butter. It was as dark a night as there could be at sea. The moonlight was masked by a layer of clouds, as were the stars. No lanterns illuminated the vessel's deck, which was unusual given the murky evening, but then it was also unusual for the captain to be up and steering the ship himself at such a late hour.

It was Iceland, an island home to many mysterious creatures, which kept the captain from his rest. With the lack of light, it was invisible from where he stood, but he knew the island was just off to port. He'd heard tales of the *huldufólk*, the hidden people, devilish tricksters who dwelled in the cliffs and toyed with any humans who crossed their paths. There was also the Lagarfljótsormurinn, a giant lake serpent who lived in the depths of Lagarfljót, breaking the surface only to dine on terrified animals and, occasionally, an unsuspecting villager. But these creatures were not his concern. The beings he feared inhabited the cave of Reynisfjall, a mountain that ended in a vast beach where the sand was black as pitch. A beach that happened to be the very one his ship was passing by.

His plan of stealthily slipping past the coast had worked well so far. He'd kept the ship's lanterns dark to avoid the light of the flames being seen from shore and, apart from the lookout, had sent his crew below to rest. Now the only sounds emanating from the schooner were the occasional creaks and groans of the rigging. *Just a while longer,* he thought, *and we'll be beyond the island's south shore.*

The night wore on, and the captain saw the cloud cover beginning to dissipate, faint traces of moonlight stretching down to dance on the sea's surface. He took in the beauty of the water's movement and admired the way light reflected on the ever-moving ocean. Strangely, though, just over the lapping of the waves, he heard a different sound coming from the depths. It began as a faint burble and quickly grew to a rush, as if a great deal of water was falling from a height.

"Rocks dead ahead!" came a sudden call from the crow's nest, and the captain felt his blood turn to ice. There were no rocks here.

"Captain, we're gonna hit 'em!" screamed the lookout, the words barely escaping his mouth before the bow collided with something enormous. The captain stared aghast at two trolls emerging from the deep, the sea pouring off their heads as they rose to their full, terrifying height.

"All hands on deck!" barked the captain as the lookout rang the bell. The sailors began streaming up from below, most in their long johns and each wondering if they were still dreaming when they saw the pair of monsters before them. Giant hands grasped the ship's bow, and the crew was knocked off their feet as the vessel suddenly lurched forward when the trolls turned it toward the shore.

The crew hurried to man the guns and didn't wait for the captain's command before they began firing. The ammunition had little effect on the massive creatures, and they continued to drag the vessel to their cave.

The captain racked his brain, searching for some piece of information that would help defeat the trolls. He could come up with only one idea, the sun, which he'd heard would turn the monsters to stone. It wasn't long until dawn now, but they'd have to slow down the trolls to stand a chance of making it until the light breached the horizon.

"Drop the anchors!" the captain yelled, and his men complied. As the mighty weights hit bottom, the chains pulled taut and the ship was secured, at least for the time being. The beasts pulled harder, the ship's frame groaning from the stress, but it stayed in place. Still, the trolls would not relent. They put the thick chains between their enormous teeth and began to gnaw, aiming to separate the ship from its anchors.

The captain realized that this was, perhaps, his crew's only chance to evacuate, and so he ordered the lifeboats lowered into the water at once. "Abandon ship!" he cried. The sailors scurried over the great boat's side into the skiffs and rowed for their lives. The trolls broke through the chains, releasing the anchors, and, realizing their meal was now scattered across smaller boats, started after the crew. The terrified men moved the oars through the water as quickly as they could, but the trolls, dragging the great ship behind them, gained on them. When they were only a few feet away, the brave captain said a quick prayer and brandished his sword as the trolls reached toward his boat, licking their lips.

Then, suddenly, the beasts froze. The sailors had held them off long enough that the first rays of sunrise had hit the water and the trolls, as well as the mighty schooner still clasped in their hands, turning them instantly to stone. Exhausted but relieved, the captain and his crew rowed their way to safety, leaving the petrified monsters and ship behind.

They are still there, and today the troll rocks and the ship are known collectively as Reynisdrangar. You can see them jutting out of the sea from the shore of the black sand beach of Reynisfjara on Iceland's south coast. Reynisfjara is also home to the Hálsanefshellir sea cave and the Gardar cliff, made up of basalt columns that together look like a massive pipe organ just the right size for giant trolls to play.

ANTWERP

BELGIUM

The city along the Scheldt River had long been a bustling, prosperous place, with hundreds of merchant ships sailing through its idyllic waters every week. The passage was easy to navigate because it was wide and deep, and the countryside surrounding it was so beautiful it inspired artists to paint it and writers to compose poetry about it. The area enjoyed an excellent reputation among traders and, overall, everyone who lived there or passed through on business was very happy.

Now this was during a time when giants were still very common, and one day, an enormous fellow named Druon Antigonus decided to build himself a castle along the riverbank. The local people didn't mind at first—castles can add a lot of charm to the landscape—but then Druon asked everyone to assemble in the town square.

"Today, I'm here to tell you that things are going to be changing around this town," he said gruffly. "From now on, any ship that passes along the Scheldt has to pay me a fee. Try to skirt around my castle without giving me a toll, and I'll have to take payment in another form and chop off the hands of the offender and throw them in the river." And with that, he marched out of town and back to his castle.

Well, everyone was incredibly upset about this and, sure enough, the next day there were guards at Antigonus's castle watching for ships and ready to collect payment. Word quickly spread to foreign traders about the tax and the terrible threat. Sailors nicknamed the Flemish city *hand werpen* ("hand throw"), and soon no one would come within fifty miles of the place. Without the business, the city fell on hard times and even the duke of Brabant, who oversaw the region, was at a loss for how to fix the problem of the giant.

That is, until one day a soldier named Silvius Brabo was walking by Antigonus's castle when he noticed a little window that might allow him to sneak in undetected. Brabo was convinced the giant was full of hot air, hiding behind his castle walls and paying his goons to do the dirty work of enforcing his dreadful toll. He felt sure that if he could confront Antigonus without the protection of his guards, he could defeat him. But he'd need help. Brabo went to the duke, and together they devised a plan.

At midnight the following evening, the duke's army sneaked through the forest and, on his command, charged the castle gate, battering it down with ship masts. As they predicted, all the castle guards ran toward the entrance to fight the duke's men, and so Brabo was able to climb up the side of the castle and through the window undetected.

There, he found Antigonus hiding. Upon seeing Brabo, however, the giant grabbed his club and swung it at the soldier with all his might. But Brabo was quicker, and, with three slashes of his sword, he cut off the giant's head and hands and threw them into the river.

The city rejoiced and hailed Brabo as a hero. The victory party in the town square lasted all the following day and into the next evening. Everyone was in a festive mood, excited to spread the word of the town's liberation.

"Let's get rid of this horrible *hand werpen* nickname and come up with a new name for ourselves," suggested one of the town's elders.

"No," said the duke. "Let's keep the name as a reminder of our victory as we ask the merchants back *an 't werf* (at the wharf). And let's make the Antwerp coat of arms a castle with two hands raised above it." Everyone cheered, and so it is to this day.

The castle on the Scheldt River, now known as Het Steen, is still there, having been rebuilt over the years. And, in front of Antwerp City Hall, you'll find the Brabo Fountain that depicts the battle in which the brave soldier freed the city from a giant's tyranny. At the very top is Brabo the Brave grasping Antigonus's severed hand, preparing to hurl it into the water.

ICEBERG ALLEY

CANADA

The morning began in the usual way for the villagers of Ferryland. They shut off their alarm clocks, sleepily pulled themselves out of their cozy beds, and headed to their kitchens to make breakfast. But, as they sipped their coffee and peered out their windows, they discovered their view had radically changed overnight. In the bay where there had been nothing but water before was now an enormous iceberg. It was bigger than three houses stacked on top of each other and one of the largest any of them had ever seen. And that was really saying something, for the people of Ferryland live along Iceberg Alley.

Iceberg Alley, so named because it's one of the best places in the world for spotting the frozen leviathans, is a bustling place come spring as new bergs break away from the glaciers of western Greenland and the Canadian Arctic and float south along the North Atlantic passageway. They travel over eighteen thousand miles along the coastline of Labrador and the island of Newfoundland, arriving in every shape and color, from bright white to sparkling aquamarine. The average iceberg is the size of a fifteen-story building, and some are so large they can be seen from outer space.

The Newfoundlanders greet the frosty visitors warmly, heading out on their boats to get a closer look (but not too close—the frozen blocks above the water are just the tips of the icebergs, with 90 percent of their mass lying beneath the water's surface, which could spell trouble for any vessel's hull). Somewhere between four hundred and eight hundred icebergs usually float by each season—so many that the islanders put them to good use, drinking the ten-thousand-year-old water and even using it to brew Iceberg Beer. The frozen giants are constantly on the move at a speed of about half a mile per hour, so every day the landscape of the sea changes as the bergs make their way out to the open ocean.

Visitors can see the icebergs during a picnic along the shore, which is home to colonies of puffins and over 350 other species of birds. You can also get up close by boat or kayak, or even go diving for a view of the bergs beneath the waves. Keep your eyes peeled for the thousands of humpback whales that swim along the alley and the shipwrecks that line the coast.

AVENUE OF THE BAOBABS

MADAGASCAR

If you travel to the African island of Madagascar and find yourself on the remote dirt road that connects the towns of Morondava and Belon'i Tsiribihina, you'll be forgiven for wondering if you've somehow done a headstand without knowing it. For, right in front of you, towering almost a hundred feet in the air, are trees that appear to be growing upside down.

This is the Avenue of the Baobabs, home to the odd-looking dendrologic colossuses known in Malagasy as *reniala*, "mother of the forest." Their broad, flat canopies spread out like roots reaching toward the sky and their trunks are as wide as an African elephant measured from the tip of its trunk to the end of its tail. These trees are incredibly useful—their fruit is rich with nutrients, and the fiber from their bark can be turned into rope, cloth, or even strings for musical instruments. The bark also has the amazing ability to grow back if it's been removed. The baobabs' trunks can store more than thirty thousand gallons of water, which is why they're also sometimes called Bottle Trees.

No one is sure quite how long these monarchs of the forest have been here (they don't have the usual tree rings to count, so it's impossible to tell exactly how old they are). One tale goes that upon seeing its fat trunk and rough, red bark reflected in a pond for the first time, the baobab complained so loudly and so frequently about not being as attractive as other trees that eventually God couldn't stand the noise any longer and replanted the baobab upside down. No longer bothered by its looks because its head was in the ground, the tree never complained again.

It is a bit of a shame we can't hear what they have to say. Think of all the animals that have sat in their branches, all the people who have come to them for shade or sustenance. These trees are among the first living things the light touches each dawn and the last to say good night to the sun. Imagine what stories they'd have to tell, what lessons we might learn.

HANG SƠN ĐOÒNG

VIETNAM

Not so very long ago, in the year 1991, a young man named Hồ Khanh was searching the jungle near Phong Nha-Ke Bang National Park in Vietnam for firewood when he saw a storm approaching. He took shelter in the opening of a cave and waited for the weather to pass, but as he stood there, he heard a mighty wind and a rushing river behind him. *A cave that could produce such noises must be enormous,* he thought, as he peered deeper into its dark mouth. He couldn't make out much through the blackness and didn't dare push deeper into the cavity without a light or ropes, so he went back to his village and vowed to return and investigate further. But when he tried to find it again, Hồ Khanh could not retrace his steps through the wild tropical forest. Years passed and he went back to his life of farming, wondering whether he would ever find the cave again.

Then one day, a team of professional explorers arrived in the region and, having heard the story of Hồ Khanh's incredible cave, asked him to join their expedition. The group searched and searched, discovering many other beautiful caves along the way. Still, the giant cavern eluded them. Hồ Khanh was determined, though, and one cold morning, eighteen years after he had first discovered it, he once again came across a cave entrance where he heard the churning of a river and the roar of wind emerging from a place deep below the ground. He had found it and, along with the team of explorers, finally made his way into the mysterious depths below.

They had found the largest cave in the world. A river does indeed flow through it and helped form the giant cavern, believed to be between two million and five million years old. The series of chambers twists and turns for more than five miles, and, in some spots, it's wide enough to fly a jumbo jet through and tall enough to house a forty-story skyscraper.

They named it Hang Sơn Đoòng, meaning "cave of the mountain river," and within its depths the group uncovered a 230-foot stalagmite, which they called Hand of Dog because it reminded them of a giant dog's paw. Further on they saw that part of the cave ceiling had collapsed so that sunlight streamed in and vegetation grew. The mammoth rock formations and lush greenery felt so ancient, like something from prehistoric times, that the group named the spot Watch Out for Dinosaurs. Continuing on, they discovered a second and even larger forest, dubbed the Garden of Edam, where giant ferns reach toward the misty sunlight and trees grow nearly a hundred feet high, the perfect perches for monkeys and birds.

Today, a small number of visitors can explore the cave with guides and camp within the massive cavern. The trip is difficult and not for the faint of heart, but you'll be rewarded with an experience unlike any other on the planet.

MATTERHORN

SWITZERLAND AND ITALY

nce upon a time, near what is now the border of Italy and Switzerland, there lay a verdant valley, a beautiful place with burbling streams and meadows covered in wildflowers all the colors of the rainbow. It was peaceful and safe. Shepherds tending their sheep worried so little about anything bad happening that they spent most of their time lawn bowling, using wheels of cheese or balls of butter to knock down the pins. The reason they had so little to fear was because the valley was also home to a friendly giant who watched over the land and its people. His name was Gargantua.

Gargantua, or "Old Gargy," as his friends knew him, was one of the largest giants on the planet at that time. In fact, the term *gargantuan*, which is used to describe very large, lumbering things, relates to him. He was so tall that when he stood upright he could wear the clouds as a hat, which he frequently did (much to the amusement of the valley's citizens). He laughed often, his deep guffaws rolling across the land like the booms of a thunderstorm, and if he sneezed, the force created a wind that had been known to knock down even deep-rooted trees.

If Gargantua had one fault, it was his clumsiness. Given his size, the slightest trip and fall was capable of changing the landscape. One such incident occurred in the northern part of the valley, along a solid rock ridge that went on as far as the eye could see. No one had ever seen what lay on the other side. The cloud cover to the north was so thick and elevated, even Gargantua could not see over it. One day, he decided he *had* to know.

He started over, stepping one of his giant feet across the top of the ridge. His legs were just long enough to reach the ground on either side if he stood on his tippy toes. However, when Gargantua tried to swing his other leg over, he lost his balance. Down he fell, crashing with a force so great that it flattened the ridge. And while Gargantua was okay, only one piece of the mountain—a jagged peak shaped like the triangular section between the giant's legs—remained.

The peak he created is still there, rising 14,692 feet into the air, and is known as the Matterhorn, a name made from the German words *matte* (meadow) and *horn* (peak). The beautiful Aosta Valley of Italy remains, too, now separated from its neighbor, the town of Zermatt in the Mattertal Valley of Switzerland, only by Gargantua's mountain. Happily, the people who lived in the valleys on both sides found they had a mutual love of alpine sports, and today you can still ski from Switzerland to Italy and back again during a trip to the Matterhorn (or Monte Cervino, as it's known in Italian).

ANGKOR

CAMBODIA

It was a hot and humid morning in the early twelfth century as Suryavarman II, king of Cambodia's Khmer Empire, made his way through the capital city of Angkor on elephant back. He waved to his subjects as he passed by, basking in their admiration for him, the warrior king known as the Shield of the Sun who, at just fourteen years old, had seized the throne from his uncle after ambushing his caravan.

Many years of a glorious reign had passed since then, but Suryavarman II wanted to be sure his legacy was secure, and he was certain his new temple would do the trick. As he arrived at the monument, stopping at the Elephant Gate to dismount from his pachyderm, he couldn't help but be impressed with Angkor Wat.

The massive laterite and sandstone complex was a masterpiece, if he did say so himself. Built in honor of the Hindu god Vishnu, it was the largest temple ever constructed in the city. The design was inspired by Mount Meru, the legendary home of the gods, and at the center stood five grand towers rising more than two hundred feet into the air, collectively known as the Temple Mountain. It was surrounded by courtyards and galleries decorated with bas-relief scenes from Hindu epics, battles between demons and *devas*, as well as one mural that was the king's personal favorite: a depiction of a great parade of soldiers, courtiers, and subjects, with him at the center. There was even a giant moat running around the entire complex.

There was still a bit more work to do before it was completed, but by Suryavarman II's calculation, it would be finished by the time he returned from this next military campaign. After a last look at his incredible temple, he mounted his elephant and went to join his army for the march off to war.

Unfortunately, dear readers, Suryavarman II never returned to Angkor, having met his end during the battle. But Angkor Wat's stone spires still jut up from the tropical forest of Cambodia, and its murals of the gods and Suryavarman II are there for you to see.

Nearby you can also explore more incredible temples built by other Khmer kings during the country's Golden Age. Ta Prohm temple was swallowed up by the jungle and now has enormous tree roots running along its walls. At Bayon temple, 54 towers decorated with 216 enormous faces carved in stone peer down at visitors, while Preah Khan features 72 *garudas*, birdlike creatures, holding serpents known as *nagas*.

But, as Suryavarman II had hoped, none rival the grandeur of Angkor Wat, which at 402 acres remains one of the largest religious monuments in the world today and even appears on the national flag of Cambodia.

DARK HEDGES

NORTHERN IRELAND

Long ago there lived a man named James Stuart who resided with his family on a large estate nestled in the green hills of the Irish countryside. James had inherited the estate from his father, Irwin, who had inherited it from his father, who was also named James, who had inherited it from his father, William, who had inherited it from his relative, who was also named James, who had received the estate as a gift from the king, who was (you guessed it) yet another James.

But the James of this story is the one who, in 1775, built a luxurious mansion on the estate and dubbed it "Gracehill House" in honor of his wife, Grace, whom he liked very much. Because the house was so opulent, he thought it only fitting that the drive leading up to it was also grand, and so James planted an allée of more than 150 beech trees along Bregagh Road. The effect was impressive, indeed, and as guests arrived for one grand affair or another they marveled at the sight, just as James had hoped they would.

But rather mysteriously, the trees on either side began arching across the road toward one another. Their branches intertwined, creating a tangled tunnel, and, as time passed, the canopy grew thicker and thicker. The gnarled passage was covered in shadows, even on sunny days, and those who traveled along it stopped calling the road by its proper name. Instead, it became known as the Dark Hedges and strange tales began to emerge that persist to this day.

After nightfall, many report seeing a specter, the Grey Lady, gliding across Bregagh Road. There, she darts in and out of the ancient, gnarled Hedges, following travelers until they pass the last beech tree, then vanishes into thin air. Some say she's a ghost of a maid who passed away at a nearby house under mysterious circumstances; others think she's the ghost of James Stuart's daughter Margaret, who had the ominous nickname "Cross Peggy." Whoever she is, the Grey Lady appears on dark nights throughout the year, but on Halloween, it's said she's joined by the ghosts of the other tormented souls buried in an abandoned graveyard in a nearby field. On this spooky night, those brave enough to call out a greeting might consider, "Hello, James!" One of the spirits is bound to answer.

M.A.G.I.C.
TIPS FOR TRAVELING

When I was a young person just starting out on my travels, I met a wise old wizard walking along the White Cliffs of Dover (which, some say, are white because a giant's ship once got stuck between them when it tried to sail through the narrowest part of the English Channel between Calais and Dover. His crew soaped the sides of the boat, and it managed to slip through, but so much of the soap was scraped onto the cliffs that they turned white. The waves at the base remain particularly foamy, too). This old wizard had been to every corner of the earth by the time I met him, and, as we shared the road for a while, he passed along the following advice for adventuring. It has served me well over the years, and, dear readers, I hope it will do the same for you.

Mind the rules and warnings put in place by explorers who've come before you. They'll keep you and the land you're visiting safe.

Always leave a place as you found it so that those who come after you can enjoy it, too. (I have on good authority from a sorceress friend that people who don't are cursed with bad weather whenever they travel from then on.)

Go with an open mind and a curious heart. They will serve you as well as any guidebook.

In the moment is the best place to be.

Chocolate. Always travel with some. Sharing a piece is universally accepted as a sign of friendship, and it has even been known to satisfy a hungry troll just long enough for you to scamper away.

PHOTO CREDITS

BIBLIOGRAPHY

The following books, articles, websites, and videos were incredibly helpful in my research and are great places to start should you want to know more. I've also included notes about alternative myths and legends I've encountered for some of the destinations named in this book because, with lore, there is often more than one version of a story.

ANGKOR

Higham, Charles. *The Civilization of Angkor*. Oakland: University of California Press, 2001.

National Geographic: Engineering the Impossible, season 2, episode 4, "Angkor Wat." Directed by Sally Aitken, Kelly McClughan, and James Wilkes, written by Sally Aitken, Maija Leivo, and Gilbert Reid. National Geographic Society, 2007.

Ray, Nick, and Greg Bloom. "Temples of Angkor." In *Cambodia*. London: Lonely Planet, 2012.

"Siem Reap." The Ministry of Tourism of Cambodia. www.tourismcambodia.org/provinces/47 /siem-reap/. Retrieved March 2019.

UNESCO World Heritage Centre. "Angkor." https://whc.unesco.org/en/list/668. Retrieved March 2019.

ANTWERP

Griffis, William Elliot. "Brabo and the Giant." In *Dutch Fairy Tales for Young Folks*, 139–146. New York: Thomas Y. Crowell Company, 1918. www.archive.org/details /dutchfairytalesf00grif/.

Mason, Antony. "Het Steen." In *DK Eyewitness Travel Guide Belgium and Luxembourg*. London: Dorling Kindersley, 2017.

McDonald, George. "The Hand of Antwerp." In *Frommer's Brussels & Bruges with Ghent & Antwerp*. 2nd ed., 189. Hoboken, NJ: Wiley, 2005. www.archive.org/details /brusselsbrugeswi00mcdo.

Room, Adrian. "Antwerp." In *Placenames of the World: Origins and Meanings*, 32, 428. Jefferson, NC: McFarland & Company, 1997. www.archive.org/details /placenamesofworl00room/.

Rose, Carol. "Antigonus." In *Giants, Monsters & Dragons: An Encyclopedia of Folklore, Legend, and Myth*. New York: W. W. Norton, 2000.

AVENUE OF THE BAOBABS

"The Baobab: A Malagasy Tree." Madagascar's Ministry of Tourism. www.madagascar -tourisme.com/en/what-to-do/fauna-and-flora/baobab/. Retrieved April 2019.

Parker, Edward, and Anna Lewington. "Baobab." In *Ancient Trees: Trees That Live for a Thousand Years*. Kindle ed. London: Batsford, 2012.

CAPPADOCIA

"Cappadocia." Turkish Heritage Travel. www.goreme.com/. Retrieved January 2019.

"Cappadocia: Fairy Chimneys beyond Dreams." Turkey, www.hometurkey.com/en /destinations/cappadocia/. Retrieved January 2019.

"Escape to Turkey's Otherworldly Landscape." National Geographic. www.nationalgeographic.com/travel/world-heritage/cappadocia/. Retrieved December 2018.

"Göreme National Park and the Rock Sites of Cappadocia." World Heritage List, UNESCO World Heritage Centre. https://whc.unesco.org/en/list/357. Retrieved January 2019.

Heller, Chris. "Turkey's 'Fairy Chimneys' Were Millions of Years in the Making." Smithsonian.com, September 21, 2015. www.smithsonianmag.com/travel /fairy-chimneys-turkey-180956654/.

Pasha-Robinson, Lucy. "Inside the Incredible Underground City That Once Housed 20,000 People." *The Independent* (London), December 15, 2016. www.independent.co.uk/news /world/middle-east/turkey-underground-lost-city-discovery-derinkuyu-turkey -cappadocia-a7477061.html/.

CHOCOLATE HILLS

There are a few creation stories surrounding the Chocolate Hills. A more tragic version revolves around a romance in which a giant fell in love with a mortal. When she passed away, he wept, his tears drying to form the mounds of the Chocolate Hills.

"The Chocolate Hills in Bohol, Philippines." Islands of the Philippines, April 21, 2018. https://www.islandsofthephilippines.com/2018/04/chocolate-hills-bohol-philippines/.

Sewell, Abby. "Soar Over the Otherworldly Chocolate Hills." National Geographic, June 6, 2018. www.nationalgeographic.com/travel/destinations/asia/philippines /bohol-chocolate-hills-natural-wonder/.

Woods, Michael, and Mary B. "The Chocolate Hills." In *Seven Natural Wonders of Asia and the Middle East.* Minneapolis, MN: Twenty-First Century Books, 2009. www.archive.org /details/sevennaturalwond0000wood_n9l6/.

DARK HEDGES

"The Dark Hedges." Causeway Coast & Glens Heritage Trust. www.ccght.org/darkhedges/. Retrieved November 2018.

"History." Gracehill House. www.gracehillhouse.com/history/. Retrieved November 2018.

DINAS EMRYS

According to another legend, Myrddin hid a treasure in a cave at Dinas Emrys. It's said that when the rightful person draws near, a bell will ring and the cave will be revealed. But those for whom the treasure is not meant should be wary if they go looking for it. According to local lore, one young man from nearby Beddgelert was chased away by supernatural noises and a vicious thunder and lightning storm that appeared as soon as he began to dig.

"Beddgelert, Dinas Emrys and the Welsh Princes." Beddgelert Tourism Association. https://www.beddgelerttourism.com/Dinas-Emrys-Princes/. Retrieved April 2019.

"Dinas Emrys." Land of Legends, Literature Wales. www.landoflegends.wales/theme/king -arthur/. Retrieved March 2019.

"The Legend of the Welsh Dragon." Visit Wales. https://www.visitwales.com/info/history -heritage-and-traditions/dragon-spirit-legend-welsh-dragon. Retrieved March 2019.

"The Legendary Trail of Dinas Emrys." National Trust. www.nationaltrust.org.uk/craflwyn -and-beddgelert/trails/the-legendary-trail-of-dinas-emrys/. Retrieved March 2019.

Nennius. "40-43." *History of the Britons (Historia Brittonum)*, translated by J. A. Giles, 1848. www.archive.org/details/Nennius-HistoryOfTheBritonshistoriaBrittonum/.

Rose, Carol. "Ddraig Goch, Y." In *Giants, Monsters & Dragons: An Encyclopedia of Folklore, Legend, and Myth.* New York: W. W. Norton, 2000.

"A Tale of Two Dragons." National Trust. www.nationaltrust.org.uk/craflwyn-and-beddgelert /features/a-tale-of-two-dragons/. Retrieved March 2019.

DUNVEGAN CASTLE AND GARDENS

There are several stories as to the origin of the Fairy Flag of Dunvegan and how it came to Clan MacLeod, but in all of them the flag is a gift from the fairies and can be used three times in emergencies. Also, accounts differ about when it has been waved before. The story included here combines elements of several traditions documented by R. C. MacLeod and a version recounted by the Associated Clan MacLeod Societies.

Dunvegan Castle & Gardens. www.dunvegancastle.com/. Retrieved October 2018.

"The Fairy Flag." The Associated Clan MacLeod Societies. https://clanmacleod.org/about
-macleods/the-fairy-flag.html/. Retrieved October 2018.

MacLeod, Roderick Charles. "The Fairy Flag." In *The MacLeods of Dunvegan from the Time
of Leod to the End of the Seventeenth Century.* Edinburgh: Privately printed for the Clan
MacLeod Society, 1927. www.archive.org/details/macleodsofdunveg00macl/.

FAIRY TALE ROUTE

Allan, David G. "On the Trail of Hansel and Gretel in Germany." *New York Times*, June 24,
2010. www.nytimes.com/2010/06/27/travel/27journeys-1.html/.

Denecke, Ludwig. "Brothers Grimm." *Encyclopaedia Britannica.* www.britannica.com
/biography/Brothers-Grimm/. Retrieved November 2018.

Deutsche Märchen Straße (German Fairy Tale Route). www.deutsche-maerchenstrasse
.com/en/. Retrieved November 2018.

Grimm, Jacob, and Wilhelm Grimm. *The Complete Grimm's Fairy Tales.* Kindle ed., 2018.
(Original work published 1857).

"Little Red Riding Hood. Traditional Schwalm Costume." Germany Travel. www.germany
.travel/en/towns-cities-culture/traditions-and-customs/arts-and-crafts/traditional
-schwalm-costume.html/. Retrieved November 2018.

Märchenland Reinhardswald. www.reinhardswald.de/. Retrieved February 2019.

GÁSADALUR

"Bøur to Gásadalur." Visit Faroe Islands. www.visitfaroeislands.com/place/boeur-gasadalur/.
Retrieved September 2018.

Visit Vágar. www.visitvagar.fo/. Retrieved September 2018.

GIANT'S CAUSEWAY

*Finn McCool—also known as Fionn Mac Cumhaill—is the star of many epic Irish myths and there is
another version of this story, too, in which Finn falls in love with a giantess on the island of Staffa
and builds the Causeway so that she can join him (though she doesn't in the end).*

Carroll, Ann. *The Story of the Giant's Causeway.* Kindle ed. Dublin: Poolbeg Press, 2013.

"Causeway Story: Myths & Legends." Giant's Causeway, National Trust.
www.giantscausewaytickets.com/finn-mccool/. Retrieved December 2018.

"The Giant's Causeway." Tourism Ireland. www.ireland.com/en-us/amazing-places
/giants-causeway/. Retrieved December 2018.

"Giant's Causeway and Causeway Coast." World Heritage List, UNESCO World Heritage
Centre. https://whc.unesco.org/en/list/369. Retrieved December 2018.

Giant's Causeway Official Guide. www.giantscausewayofficialguide.com/.
Retrieved December 2018.

Jones, Richard. "Giant's Causeway." In *Myths and Legends of Britain and Ireland.* London:
New Holland Publishers, 2012.

Mulraney, Frances. "The Myths and Legends of the Giant's Causeway." IrishCentral, June 29,
2016. www.irishcentral.com/travel/the-myths-and-legends-of-the-giants-causeway-photos/.

GREAT BLUE HOLE

"Belize Barrier Reef Reserve System." World Heritage List, UNESCO World Heritage Centre.
https://whc.unesco.org/en/list/764. Retrieved November 2018.

"Blue Hole." Travel Belize. www.travelbelize.org/blue-hole/. Retrieved December 2018.

Cousteau, Jacques-Yves, and Philippe Diolé. *Three Adventures: Galápagos, Titicaca, the Blue
Holes,* translated by J. F. Bernard, 153–194. New York: Doubleday, 1973. www.archive.org
/details/threeadventures00jacq/.

Cousteau, Jacques-Yves, and Rod Serling. *The Undersea World of Jacques Cousteau,* "Secrets
of the Sunken Caves." Released March 19, 1971. Metromedia Productions. YouTube video,
48:42. Posted April 24, 2014. www.youtube.com/watch?v=hM9pa5JQmz0.

GREAT SPHINX OF GIZA

David, Rosalie. "Everyday Life." *Handbook to Life in Ancient Egypt*. Rev. ed. New York: Facts on File, 2003. www.archive.org/details/HandbookToLifeInAncientEgypt/.

"Dream Stela." Harvard Semitic Museum, Harvard University. www.semiticmuseum.fas .harvard.edu/dream-stela/. Retrieved November 2018.

Glassman, Gary. "The Dream Stela of Thutmosis IV." *Nova*, aired December 31, 2009. Corporation for Public Broadcasting. www.pbs.org/wgbh/nova/article/sphinx-stela/.

Hadingham, Evan. "Uncovering Secrets of the Sphinx." *Smithsonian Magazine*, February 2010, www.smithsonianmag.com/history/uncovering-secrets-of-the-sphinx-5053442/.

Haughton, Brian. "The Mystery of the Great Sphinx." *Ancient History Encyclopedia*, June 1, 2011. www.ancient.eu/article/236/the-mystery-of-the-great-sphinx/.

McDevitt, April. "The Prince and the Sphinx." Ancient Egypt: The Mythology. www.egyptianmyths.net/mythsphinx.htm/. Retrieved November 2018.

Spence, Lewis. "The Dream of Thothmes." In *Myths & Legends of Ancient Egypt*, 85–86. London: George G. Harrap & Company, 1915. www.archive.org/details /MythsAnLegendsOfAncientEgypt/.

HANG SƠN ĐOÒNG

"The Biggest Cave in the World." VietNamNet Bridge, Public Radio International, July 6, 2009. www.pri.org/stories/2009-07-06/biggest-cave-world.

Edström, Martin. "Sơn Đoòng 360." National Geographic. www.nationalgeographic .com/news-features/son-doong-cave/2/#s=pano48. Retrieved November 2018.

Evans-Butler, Sam, and David Jaffe. "Photo Essay: Inside Son Doong, the World's Largest Cave." *Condé Nast Traveler*, June 20, 2018. www.cntraveler.com/gallery /photos-inside-son-doong-the-worlds-largest-cave.

Jenkins, Mark. "Conquering an Infinite Cave." National Geographic, January 2011. www.nationalgeographic.com/magazine/2011/01/vietnam-cave.

ICEBERG ALLEY

Leveille, David. "A Tiny Canadian Town Has a New Best Friend: This Massive, Gorgeous Iceberg." Public Radio International, April 19, 2017. www.pri.org/stories/2017-04-19 /tiny-canadian-town-has-new-best-friend-massive-gorgeous-iceberg/.

Mallonee, Laura. "An Enormous Hunk of Ice Gets Stuck in Iceberg Alley." *Wired*, April 21, 2017. www.wired.com/2017/04/enormous-hunk-ice-gets-stuck-iceberg-alley/.

Newfoundland and Labrador Tourism. www.newfoundlandlabrador.com/. Retrieved February 2019.

IZTACCÍHUATL AND POPOCATÉPETL

There are many versions of this tale. In some, Popoca is an Aztec warrior sent to battle rival groups, and in others, he is a Tlaxcalan warrior fighting the Aztecs. Sometimes Izta's father sends Popoca to war in anger, and other times he does so in order to raise his future son-in-law's profile. In all of them, though, Izta is lied to by a rival of Popoca, and when he returns from battle, he watches over his lover until they are transformed into volcanoes. In this retelling, I've weaved in another beautiful Aztec legend of Quetzalcóatl and the rabbit, which tells how the moon came to have a hare-shaped mark on its surface.

Burguete, Maria, informant. Collected by Nico Williamson. "*La Leyenda de la Luna*—the Legend of the Moon." USC Digital Folklore Archives, May 1, 2017. http://folklore.usc.edu/?p=37672/.

"The Most Romantic Mexican Legends." México, September 2, 2018. www.mexico.mx/en /articles/leyendas-romanticas-mexicanas/.

Myth, Mortals, and Immortality: Works from Museo Soumaya de México (exhibit guide). Smithsonian Latino Center, September 13–November 2, 2006. www.latino.si.edu/PDF /Mexico%20Exhibit.pdf/.

Nahuatl Dictionary. University of Oregon, https://nahuatl.uoregon.edu/. Retrieved May 2019.

Orozco, Chela. "The Legend of Popocatépetl and Iztaccíhuatl: A Love Story." Inside Mexico, March 8, 2019. www.inside-mexico.com/the-legend-of-popocatepetl-iztaccihuatl/.

Ramírez, Edna. *The Rabbit on the Moon*. Wyndmoor, PA: Mermaid Spirits Publishing, 2017.

Tonatiuh, Duncan. *The Princess and the Warrior: A Tale of Two Volcanoes*. Kindle ed. New York: Abrams Books for Young Readers, 2016.

Vitaliano, Dorothy B. *Legends of the Earth: Their Geologic Origins*. Bloomington: Indiana University Press, 1973: 123.

KNOSSOS

Glaves, Rachel. "Knossos: Journey to the Centre of the Labyrinth." Current World Archaeology, October 23, 2018. www.world-archaeology.com/travel /knossos-journey-to-the-centre-of-the-labyrinth/.

Guerber, H. A. "The Minotaur." In *The Myths of Greece & Rome*. London: George G. Harrap & Company, 1907. www.archive.org/details/in.ernet.dli.2015.103404/.

"Knossos." Municipality of Heraklion. www.heraklion.gr/en/ourplace/knossos/knossos.html/.

Mark, Joshua J. "Theseus & the Minotaur: More Than a Myth?" *Ancient History Encyclopedia*, February 18, 2011. www.ancient.eu/article/209/theseus—the-minotaur-more-than-a-myth/.

"The Monster in the Maze." In *Great Myths and Legends*. Chicago: World Book, 1984. www.archive.org/details/greatmythslegend00worl/.

Philip, Neil. "The Minotaur." In *Myths & Legends Explained*. London: Dorling Kindersley Limited, 2007. www.archive.org/details/Myths_and_Legends_Explained_the_worlds_most _enduring_myths_and_legends_explored_/.

Searching for Lost Worlds, "Atlantis: Mystery of the Minoans." Discovery Channel, 1999. www.archive.org/details/Searching_For_Lost_Worlds_Atlantis_Discovery_Channel _WOC_1995/.

Vitaliano, Dorothy B. *Legends of the Earth: Their Geologic Origins*. Bloomington: Indiana University Press, 1973: 244.

KOMODO ISLAND

Ciofi, Claudio. "The Komodo Dragon." *Scientific American* 280, no. 3 (March 1999): 84–91.

"Komodo Dragon." National Geographic. www.nationalgeographic.com/animals/reptiles/k /komodo-dragon/. Retrieved September 2018.

"Komodo National Park." Wonderful Indonesia. www.indonesia.travel/gb/en/destinations /bali-nusa-tenggara/labuan-bajo/komodo-national-park. Retrieved September 2018.

"Komodo National Park." World Heritage List, UNESCO World Heritage Centre. https://whc.unesco.org/en/list/609. Retrieved September 2018.

Meijer, Hanneke. "Here Be Dragons: The Million-Year Journey of the Komodo Dragon." *The Guardian* (Manchester), May 17, 2017. www.theguardian.com/science/2017/may/17 /here-be-dragons-the-million-year-journey-of-the-komodo-dragon/.

LAPLAND

"Dark Side of the Auroras—Meanings and Myths." House of Lapland. www.lapland.fi/visit /lapland-northern-lights-myths-auroras/. Retrieved November 2018.

"Lapland." Visit Finland. www.visitfinland.com/lapland/. Retrieved December 2018.

"Revontulet 'Fox Fires.'" Visit Finland. www.visitfinland.com/article/revontulet-fox-fires/. Retrieved December 2018.

LE MONT-SAINT-MICHEL

"The Archangel and the Origins of the Abbey." Centre des Monuments Nationaux. www.abbaye-mont-saint-michel.fr/en/Explore/The-archangel-and-the-origins-of-the -Abbey/. Retrieved September 2018.

Etherton, Caitlin. "Soar Over a Medieval Monastery Surrounded by Sea in This Video." National Geographic, April 16, 2018. www.nationalgeographic.com/travel/destinations /europe/france/things-to-see-mont-saint-michel/.

"A Headache at Mont-Saint-Michel." Normandy Then and Now, January 18, 2014. www.normandythenandnow.com/a-headache-at-mont-saint-michel/.

"History of the Monument." Centre des Monuments Nationaux. www.abbaye-mont -saint-michel.fr/en/Explore/L-histoire-de-l-abbaye-du-Mont-Saint-Michel/. Retrieved September 2018.

"Mont-Saint-Michel." *Encyclopaedia Britannica.* www.britannica.com/place/Mont-Saint-Michel. Retrieved September 2018.

"The Mont-Saint-Michel." Région Normandie. http://en.normandie-tourisme.fr/discover /normandy-must-sees/the-10-top-normandy-must-sees/mont-saint-michel-106-2.html. Retrieved September 2018.

"Mont-Saint-Michel and Its Bay." World Heritage List, UNESCO World Heritage Centre. https://whc.unesco.org/en/list/80. Retrieved September 2018.

LOFOTEN

In addition to Lofoten, where a Viking festival is held every August, Norway is rich with Viking history. The capital city of Oslo is home to the fantastic Viking Ship Museum. The island of Karmøy contains the settlement at Avaldsnes, the first royal seat of the country, where you'll find a fascinating living history Viking village that hosts a festival each June.

Avaldsnes. http://avaldsnes.info/. Retrieved March 2019.

Ham, Anthony. "Lofoten." *Norway.* 7th ed., Kindle ed. London: Lonely Planet, 2018.

Lofoten. www.lofoten.info/. Retrieved March 2019.

Lofotr Viking Museum. www.lofotr.no/en/. Retrieved March 2019.

Munch, Gerd Stamø, Olav Sverre Johansen, and Else Roesdahl, eds. *Borg in Lofoten. A Chieftain's Farm in North Norway*, 100–105. Trondheim, Norway: Tapir Academic Press, 2003.

Nielssen, Alf Ragnar. *Landnåm fra nord: utvandringa fra det nordlige Norge til Island i Vikingtid*, translated by Marion Fjelde Larsen, 173–178. Stamsund, Norway: Orkana Akademisk, 2012.

LOST CITY OF PETRA

Lawler, Andrew. "Reconstructing Petra." *Smithsonian Magazine*, June 2007. www.smithsonianmag.com/history/reconstructing-petra-155444564/.

"The Man Who Discovered a 'Lost' Wonder of the World." University of Cambridge, August 22, 2012. http://www.cam.ac.uk/research/news/the-man-who-discovered-a -%E2%80%98lost%E2%80%99-wonder-of-the-world.

Milstein, Mati. "Petra." National Geographic. www.nationalgeographic.com /archaeology-and-history/archaeology/lost-city-petra/. Retrieved July 2018.

Orlean, Susan. "Zooming in on Petra." *Smithsonian Magazine*, October 2018. www.smithsonian mag.com/history/petra-jordan-drone-3d-scan-digital-modeling-180970310/.

Petra (exhibition). American Museum of Natural History, October 18, 2003–July 6, 2004. www.amnh.org/exhibitions/petra/.

"Petra." Google Maps Treks. www.google.com/maps/about/behind-the-scenes/streetview /treks/petra/. Retrieved July 2018.

"Petra." Jordan Tourism Board. http://in.visitjordan.com/Wheretogo/Petra.aspx. Retrieved July 2018.

"Petra: One of 7 Wonders." Petra Development and Tourism Region Authority. http://www.visitpetra.jo/. Retrieved July 2018.

"Petra." World Heritage List, UNESCO World Heritage Centre. https://whc.unesco.org/en/list/326. Retrieved July 2018.

Sánchez, Cruz. "Petra Lost and Found." *National Geographic History*. https://www.nationalgeographic.com/archaeology-and-history/magazine/2016/01-02/petra/. Retrieved July 2018.

MATTERHORN

Griffis, William Elliot. "The Mountain Giants." In *Swiss Fairy Tales*. New York: Thomas Y. Crowell Company, 1920. www.archive.org/details/swissfairytales00grif/.

Guerber, H. A. "Legends of Vaud and Valais." In *Legends of Switzerland*. New York: Dodd, Mead and Company, 1909. https://archive.org/details/legendsofswitzer00guer/.

"Matterhorn." *Encyclopaedia Britannica*. www.britannica.com/place/Matterhorn-mountain-Europe/. Retrieved March 2019.

"Matterhorn." Zermatt Tourism. www.zermatt.ch/en/matterhorn. Retrieved March 2019.

Rey, Guido. *The Matterhorn*, translated by J. E. C. Eaton, 62–63. London: T. Fisher Unwin, 1907. www.archive.org/details/matterhorn00eatogoog/.

PIG BEACH

No one knows how the pigs of Pig Beach ended up on Big Major Cay. That they were survivors of a shipwreck is one theory, while others say they were put there by sailors who planned to come back and cook them but who never returned.

"Official Home of the Swimming Pigs." Islands of the Bahamas. www.bahamas.com/swimmingpigs/. Retrieved April 2019.

Todd, T. R. *Pigs of Paradise: The Story of the World-Famous Swimming Pigs*. Kindle ed. New York: Skyhorse Publishing, 2018.

PONTE DELLA PAGLIA

Birmingham, Brenda. "Ponte della Paglia and Bridge of Sighs." In *DK Eyewitness Travel Guide: Venice & the Veneto*, edited by Jo Bourne, Molly Perham, and Linda Williams. New York: DK Publishing, 2012. www.archive.org/details/isbn_9780756684105/.

"Doge's Palace." Fondazione Musei Civici di Venezia. www.palazzoducale.visitmuve.it/en/home/. Retrieved March 2019.

Ongania, Ferdinando, and Camillo Boito. "The Legends and Historical Records of Saint Mark." In *The Basilica of Saint Mark in Venice: Illustrated from the Points of View of Art and History*, translated by William Scott and F. H. Rosenberg Venice: Ongania, 1888–1895.

Steedman, Amy. "S. Mark and the Fisherman." *Legends and Stories of Italy for Children*. New York: G. P. Putnam's Sons, 1909. www.archive.org/details/legendsstoriesof00stee/.

"Venice and Its Lagoon." World Heritage List, UNESCO World Heritage Centre. https://whc.unesco.org/en/list/394. Retrieved March 2019.

PREDJAMA CASTLE

"The Death of Erasmus Lueger." *The Rough Guide to Slovenia*. 4th ed., Kindle ed., 207. London: Rough Guides, June 2017.

"Predjama Castle." Lonely Planet. www.lonelyplanet.com/slovenia/attractions/predjama-castle/a/poi-sig/490460/1325401/. Retrieved September 2018.

"Predjama Castle: A Fairytale Castle Embraced by Rock." Park Postojnska Jama. www.postojnska-jama.eu/en/predjama-castle/. Retrieved September 2018.

Strochlic, Nina. "What a World: Robin Hood's Secret Castle." *Daily Beast*, June 27, 2015, www.thedailybeast.com/what-a-world-robin-hoods-secret-castle/.

RAPA NUI (EASTER ISLAND)

Arnold, Caroline. *Easter Island*. New York: Clarion Books, 2000. https://archive.org/details
/easterislandgian00arno/.

McCarthy, Carolyn. "Easter Island (Rapa Nui)." *Chile & Easter Island*. London: Lonely Planet,
2009. https://archive.org/details/chileeasterislan0000mcca/.

"Mythology of Easter Island." This Is Chile. www.thisischile.cl/mythology-of-easter
-island/?lang=en/. Retrieved March 2019.

"Rapa Nui." Chile Travel. www.chile.travel/en/where-to-go/rapa-nui/. Retrieved March 2019.

"Rapa Nui National Park." World Heritage List, UNESCO World Heritage Centre,
https://whc.unesco.org/en/list/715. Retrieved March 2019.

Trachtman, Paul. "The Secrets of Easter Island." *Smithsonian Magazine*, March 2002.
www.smithsonianmag.com/history/the-secrets-of-easter-island-59989046/.

REYNISDRANGAR

"Folklore in Iceland." Guide to Iceland. www.guidetoiceland.is/history-culture/folklore
-in-iceland/. Retrieved October 2018.

Inspired by Iceland. www.inspiredbyiceland.com/. Retrieved October 2018.

"Lagarfljót." Guide to Iceland. www.guidetoiceland.is/travel-iceland/drive/lagarfljot/.
Retrieved October 2018.

SALAR DE UYUNI

Unger, Elizabeth. "These Salt Flats Are One of the Most Remarkable Vistas on Earth."
National Geographic, May 3, 2017. www.nationalgeographic.com/travel/destinations
/south-america/bolivia/how-to-see-salar-de-uyuni-salt-flats-bolivia/.

"Uyuni Salt Flat." Visit Bolivia. www.visitbolivia.org/uyuni-salt-flat.php/. Retrieved
October 2018.

SHIMANE PREFECTURE

Chamberlain, Basil Hall. *The Kojiki: Records of Ancient Matters*. Rutland, VT: C. E. Tuttle Co.,
1982.

"Okuizumo." Japanese National Tourism Organization. www.japan.travel/en/destinations
/chugoku/shimane/oku-izumo-area/. Retrieved November 2018.

Philip, Neil. "Susano, the Storm God." *Myths & Legends Explained*. London: Dorling Kindersley,
2007. www.archive.org/details/Myths_and_Legends_Explained_the_worlds_most
_enduring_myths_and_legends_explored_/.

Tarao, Seiji. *A Guide to the Mysteries of the Kojiki*, translated by Henna Valkama and Lisa Kay.
Yonago City: Ancient Izumo Kingdom Research Society, 2014.

Visit Izumo. www.izumo-kankou.gr.jp/english/. Retrieved November 2018.

Visit Shimane. www.visitshimane.com/. Retrieved November 2018.

SKELETON COAST

Bowerman, Karen. "What It's Like to Explore the Pristine Skeleton Coast of Namibia." CNN,
November 22, 2013. www.cnn.com/travel/article/namibia-skeleton-coast/.

Crook, Clive. "The Skeleton Coast." *The Atlantic*, May 2007. www.theatlantic.com/magazine
/archive/2007/05/the-skeleton-coast/305785/.

"Namib Sand Sea." World Heritage List, UNESCO World Heritage Centre.
https://whc.unesco.org/en/list/1430. Retrieved April 2018.

"Skeleton Coast Park." Ministry of Environment & Tourism Namibia.
www.met.gov.na/national-parks/skeleton-coast-park/227/. Retrieved April 2018.

Strochlic, Nina. "Namibia's Spooky Skeleton Coast." *Daily Beast*, March 5, 2014.
www.thedailybeast.com/namibias-spooky-skeleton-coast/.

"Three Shipwrecks on Namibia's Skeleton Coast." Namibia Tourism Board.
  www.namibiatourism.com.na/blog/Three-Shipwrecks-on-Namibia-s-Skeleton-Coast/.
  Retrieved February 2019.

TABLE MOUNTAIN
The Van Hunks legend tells of how Table Mountain got its "tablecloth," but there are many fascinating tales around the creation of the mountain itself. In one Xhosa tale, Table Mountain is known as Umlindi Wemingizimu (Watcher of the South), one of four giants created during a battle between the god Qamata and a sea dragon and one who still watches over this cardinal point of the planet today.

Colvin, Ian D. "How Table Mountain Got Its Cloud." In *Romance of Empire South Africa*,
  155–164. London: T. C. & E. C. Jack, 1909. www.archive.org/details/southafrica00colvrich/.
Rossetti, Dante Gabriel, *Jan Van Hunks*, edited by John Robert Wahl. New York: The New
  York Public Library, 1952. www.archive.org/details/janvanhunks00ross/.
Stewart, Dianne, and Jay Heale. "Van Hunks and the Devil." *African Myths & Legends*. Kindle
  ed. Cape Town: Struik Lifestyle, 2014.
"Table Mountain." Cape Town Tourism. www.capetown.travel/explore-cape-towns-iconic
  -table-mountain/. Retrieved January 2019.
"Table Mountain Myths and Legends." CapeTownMagazine.com, February 14, 2017.
  www.capetownmagazine.com/cape-confidential/table-mountain-myths-and-legends
  /123_22_19779/.

TAJ MAHAL
Koch, Emma. *Complete Taj Mahal and the Riverfront Gardens of Agra*. London: Thames &
  Hudson, 2012.
Qureshi, Siraj. "A Brief History of Taj Mahal, the Epitome of Love." *India Today*, July 20, 2018.
  www.indiatoday.in/save-the-taj/story/a-brief-history-of-the-taj-mahal-the-epitome
  -of-love-1290588-2018-07-19/.
"Taj Mahal." Department of Tourism, Government of Uttar Pradesh, India.
  www.tajmahal.gov.in/. Retrieved March 2019.
"Taj Mahal." History.com. www.history.com/topics/india/taj-mahal/. Retrieved March 2019.
"Taj Mahal." World Heritage List, UNESCO World Heritage Centre. https://whc.unesco.org
  /en/list/252. Retrieved March 2019.

TOWER OF LONDON
"Edward V & Richard Duke of York." Westminster Abbey. www.westminster-abbey.org
  /abbey-commemorations/royals/edward-v-richard-duke-of-york/. Retrieved October 2018.
Historic Royal Palaces. www.hrp.org.uk/. Retrieved October 2018.
Hole, Christina. *Haunted England: A Survey of English Ghost-Lore*. 2nd ed. London: B. T.
  Batsford, 1950: 60–62.
"Tower of London." World Heritage List, UNESCO World Heritage Centre.
  https://whc.unesco.org/en/list/488. Retrieved October 2018.

WAITOMO GLOWWORM CAVES
"Waitomo Glowworm Cave." Waitomo Caves Discovery Centre. www.waitomocaves.com
  /downloads/Glowworm%20Cave.pdf/. Retrieved April 2018.
"Waitomo Glowworm Caves." Discover Waitomo. https://www.waitomo.com/discover/magic
  /the-history-of-waitomo-glowworm-cave/. Retrieved April 2019.

WHITE CLIFFS OF DOVER
Guerber, H. A. "The Giant's Ship." In *Myths of the Norsemen*, 235. London: George G. Harrap
  and Co., 1908. www.archive.org/details/in.ernet.dli.2015.190990/.

Vitaliano, Dorothy B. *Legends of the Earth: Their Geologic Origins*. Bloomington: Indiana
    University Press, 1973: 79.
"The White Cliffs of Dover." National Trust. www.nationaltrust.org.uk/the-white-cliffs-of
    -dover/. Retrieved December 2018.

WIZARD ISLAND

*There are many wonderful Klamath Tribes legends about the creation of Crater Lake and Wizard
Island. The one included here is one of the most well known. In another story, the ruler of the
underworld falls in love with the daughter of a tribal chief who refuses him. In anger, he lays waste
to the land with fire until a human sacrifice is made and the chief of the aboveground forces him
back beneath the earth, filling the entrance to the underworld with water and thus creating Crater
Lake. Others tell of terrible fates befalling Klamath hunters and warriors who breached the borders
of Crater Lake, which was home to the great Spirit Chief and could not be approached by mortals
except for the medicine men of the Klamath.*
Applegate, O. C. "The Klamath Legend of La-O." *Steel Points* 1, no. 2 (January 1907): 75–76.
    http://www.craterlakeinstitute.com/online-library/wp-content/uploads/steel-points1.pdf.
    Retrieved May 2019.
Clark, Ella E. *Indian Legends of the Pacific Northwest*. Berkeley: University of California Press,
    1953: 53–63. www.archive.org/details/indianlegendsofp00clar/.
Crater Lake Institute. www.craterlakeinstitute.com/. Retrieved February 2019.
"Crater Lake." National Park Service. www.nps.gov/crla/index.htm. Retrieved February 2019.
Greene, Linda W. "Legends Surrounding Crater Lake." In *Historic Resource Study: Crater
    Lake National Park, Oregon*, by National Park Service, 34–49. Denver, CO: National Park
    Service, 1984. www.archive.org/details/historicresource00lake/.
The Klamath Tribes. www.klamathtribes.org/. Retrieved February 2019.
Lapham, Stanton C. "The Legend of Crater Lake." In *The Enchanted Lake: Mount Mazama and
    Crater Lake in Story, History and Legend*. Portland, OR: J. K. Gill Company, 1931.

YELLOW MOUNTAIN

"Huangdi." *Encyclopaedia Britannica*. www.britannica.com/topic/Huangdi/. Retrieved
    November 2018.
Mawson, Chen. "Huangshan—the Most Beautiful Mountain in China." All Roads Traveled.
    www.allroadstraveled.com/huangshan-yellow-mountains-most-beautiful-in-china.html.
    Retrieved October 2018.
McDowall, Stephen. *Qian Qianyi's Reflections on Yellow Mountain: Traces of a Late-Ming
    Hatchet and Chisel*. Hong Kong: Hong Kong University Press, 2009.
"Mount Huangshan." World Heritage List, UNESCO World Heritage Centre.
    https://whc.unesco.org/en/list/547. Retrieved October 2018.
Naquin, Susan, and Chün-Fang Yü, eds. *Pilgrims and Sacred Sites in China*. Berkeley: University
    of California Press, 1992: 247.
Pas, Julian F. "Mount Huang." In *Historical Dictionary of Taoism*. Lanham, MD: Scarecrow
    Press, 1998.

ACKNOWLEDGMENTS

I would like to thank my agent, Elizabeth Bewley, at Sterling Lord Literistic, Inc., for believing in this project from the get-go and providing sage advice throughout the publishing process; all at Running Press Kids, especially my editor, Allison Cohen, for her brilliant ideas and enthusiasm; Frances J. Soo Ping Chow, designer; Michael Clark, project editor; Christina Palaia, who copyedited this book, Trang Chuong, who fact-checked it; and my family, for their love and encouragement always.

Last but not least, thank you to all the people who support the destinations included in these pages and who assisted with my research, most especially those who dedicate themselves to protecting our world's heritage places, ensuring their stories will continue for generations to come.